MUSTANG BON FOUNDATION

These advanced practices should only be practiced after getting the appropriate transmission, and done only by practitioners with appropriate qualifications, permissions, and pith instructions. Without such qualifications, permissions, and instructions these practices can be dangerous, so do not put yourself at risk.

Enlightened Intention, The Good Spiritual Life, and Dying into Rainbow Body

ISBN: 978-1-956950-19-9

Copyright © 2023 Mustang Bon Foundation
All rights reserved. No part of this book may be reproduced without prior written permission from the publisher.

Published by Mustang Bon Foundation

First Edition

Front cover: Shardza practicing rainbow body (source unknown)

Printed and Bound in the United States of America

Layout and design by Brad Reynolds integralartandstudies.com

Enlightened Intention, The Good Spiritual Life, and Dying into Rainbow Body

DAWA DRAG-PA
(ZLA BA GRAGS PA)

Enlightened Intention, The Good Spiritual Life, and Dying into Rainbow Body

Including Translations of The Four Manners of Dying to Accomplish Rainbow Body

&

Blue Lotus Flower
The Sacred Biography of the Venerable Bon Lama,
Dawa Dragpa
(Zla ba Grags pa)

the successor to the incomparable
Shardza Tashi Gyaltsen Rinpoche
(Shar rDza bKra' shis rGyal mtshan Rinpoche)

Written By
Kalsang Tenpa Gyaltsen
(bsKal bzang bsTan pa' rGyal mtshan)

Translated under the guidance of
His Holiness the thirty-third Menri Trizin

by Geshe Sonam Gurung and Daniel P. Brown, Ph.D.

for Mustang Bon Foundation

*May the translation of these precious lineage teachings
cause the benefits from these teachings to flourish everywhere
and serve the welfare of all beings.*

Enlightened Intention, The Good Spiritual Life, and Dying into Rainbow Body

Geshe Sonam Gurung grew up in an indigenous Bon Tibetan region of Nepal, in the Pangling Village area of Central Mustang. When he was nine years old he was sent by the local Bon lama to become a monk at Menri Monastery, the seat of the indigenous Bon religion, now located in the Dolanji area of India. He spent fourteen years obtaining his Geshe degree (the equivalent of a doctoral degree in Bon spiritual studies) under the guidance of His Holiness Menri Trizin, the spiritual leader and lineage holder of the Bon and the 33rd Head Abbott of Menri Monastery. After obtaining his Geshe degree he served as treasurer, guest master, and personal assistant to His Holiness Menri Trizin at Menri Monastery. Recently, Geshe Sonam returned to the Jomsom area of Central Mustang to reestablish and spread the indigenous Bon teachings in his country of origin. Two documentaries have been made about Geshe Sonam's life and work: *Bon: From Mustang to Menri*, and a follow-up film about his return home, *Returning the Blessings*.

Daniel P. Brown, Ph.D. is an Associate Clinical Professor in Psychology, Dept. of Psychiatry, at Harvard Medical School at Beth Israel Deaconess Medical Center. He has been on the HMS faculty for 37 years, where he teaches a variety of clinical assessment and treatment courses and also a course on performance excellence for physicians, CEOs, and judges. In graduate school at the University of Chicago he studied Sanskrit, and at the University of Wisconsin he studied Tibetan, Buddhist Sanskrit, and Pali. In the 1980s he wrote *Transformations of Consciousness* with Ken Wilber and Jack Engler. He is also the author of *Pointing Out the Great Way: The Stages of Meditation in the Mahamudra Tradition*, and two books on public dialogues with H.H. the Dalai Lama. More recently, under the guidance of H.H. Menri Trizin, he and Geshe Sonam translated Bru rGyal ba g.Yung drung's *The Pith Instructions for the Stages of the Practice Sessions of Bon rDzogs Chen [Great Completion] Meditation*, and a collection of eleven advanced yogic texts, Shar rdza bKra' shis rGyal mtshan's *sKu gsum rang shar [Self-Arising Three-fold Embodiment of Enlightenment]*.

Enlightened Intention, The Good Spiritual Life, and Dying into Rainbow Body

Table of Contents

Foreword by Geshe Sonam Gurung vii

PART I – INTRODUCTION

Enlightened Intention 1

Enlightened Activity of a Practitioner During the Dying Process 2

Rainbow Body and Relics as Inspiration of Faith and Devotion 4

Rainbow Body as an Event Observed by Others 5

The Four Ways of Dying to Manifest Rainbow Body 7

The Manner of Dying Like Space 8

The Manner of Dying Like a Sky-Dancer 9

The Manner of Dying like a Forest Fire 11

The Manner of Dying like an Awareness-Holder 12

The Dying Practitioner's Enlightened Intention Manifesting as an
   Imprint on Ordinary Physical Reality as Bones and Relics 14

Enlightened Intention Manifest in This Very Lifetime; the
   Good Spiritual Life 15

Blue Lotus Flower – Sacred Biography of Zla ba Grags pa 15

PART II – TRANSLATIONS OF THE FOUR MANNERS OF DYING IN RAINBOW BODY PRACTICE

A. A selected passage from Shar rdza Rinpoche's dByings rig mdzod
[The Precious Treasury of the Expanse and Awakened Awareness] .. 19

B. 'Jam mgon Kong sprul's description of the four manners of dying in
rainbow body practice from the Shes bya mrtha' yas pa'i rgya mtsho
[Limitless Ocean of What is to be Known] 23

Table of Contents

Part III – Blue Lotus Flower – Sacred Biography of Dawa Dragpa (Zla ba Grags pa)

Blue Lotus Flower 27

1.0 His Early Life 29

1.1 His Previous Lifetimes 29

1.2 His Birth 31

1.3 How He Entered the Spiritual Life 34

1.4 The Maturation of His Spiritual Life............................37

1.5 His Practice of the Preliminary, Actual Foundational, and Concluding Practices..40

1.6 Various Initiations and Transmissions..........................42

2.0 Meditation Practice in Retreat......................................44

3.0 The Practice of the Approach and Accomplishment Stages...47

4.0 Spontaneous Songs of Realization................................54

5.0 How He Completed the Positive Qualities of the Signs of the Path..59

5.1 The Meditation Experiences and Realizations of the Path......61

5.2 Common Signs of Accomplishment.............................64

6.0 Attaining the Accomplishment 71

6.1 How the Profound Treasures Came Forth...................72

7.0 Various Visions...75

8.0 Serving the Welfare of Sentient Beings........................76

9.0 Serving the Welfare of Followers in Different Places...........79

9.1 Serving Followers in Different Places 79

9.2 Serving Meditators in the Accomplishment Lineage 84

10.0 His Departure from Life as Rainbow Body 104

Colophon 118

References 121

Acknowledgments

Our deepest appreciation to His Holiness the 33rd Menri Trizin. It is only because of his direction and guidance that the translations of the precious texts that appear in this book could be done Our deepest gratitude also to Susan Pottish for her thorough and careful copy editing of this manuscript. Our thanks also to Brad Reynolds, the type-setter, who made the production of this work possible.

Enlightened Intention, The Good Spiritual Life, and Dying into Rainbow Body

FOREWORD

I pay homage to the benevolent Root Lamas, the Precious Ones who reveal the true nature of mind, and to my teacher and root lama, His Holiness Menri Trizin, the 33rd Abbott of Menri Monastery. More than a decade ago, Dr. Daniel Brown and I were given the task by His Holiness Menri Trizin to share a number of precious teachings with a Western audience.

Under the guidance of H.H. Menri Trizin, Dr. Brown and I translated and published, through the Pointing Out the Great Way Foundation (now called the Mustang Bon Foundation), six important works capturing many of the precious Bon teachings. This seventh book was our last joint project. Before we could complete its publication, Dr. Brown passed away on April 4, 2022. The Foundation, which holds the copyright of these books, is grateful for the generous donations that supported this important work of bringing these sacred teachings to Western audiences.

This book contains two separate translations. The first is a translation of the brief instructions for achieving Rainbow Body, the culmination of Dzogchen practices, as rendered by Shardza Tashi Gyaltsen (1859 – 1934). I would like to emphasize that this esoteric, and not easy to understand, text was written for a monastic audience deeply familiar with the Bon Buddhist practices and Bon terms. These instructions have traditionally been reserved for advanced practitioners and have been handed down, often orally, to qualified students. Note that you should not attempt to practice these advanced techniques unless you are working under the instruction of a qualified Lama. The second part of this book contains a biography of the Venerable Bon Lama, Dawa Dragpa, written by Kalsang Tenpa Gyaltsen, and is a valuable resource for any student of Bon.

Regarding certain spellings, the cover of this book uses a phonetic spelling of the Tibetan names, while in the book text itself we have primarily used the traditional Wylie spelling, which is the way the Tibetan

Enlightened Intention, The Good Spiritual Life, and Dying into Rainbow Body

names were originally translated. Therefore, you will see that Lama Dawa Dragpa's name appears in the text as Zla ba Grags pa; his spiritual name appears as Kun bzang Nam mkha' sNying po, while Shardza Tashi Gyaltsen Rinpoche's name appears as Shar rDza bKra' shis rGyal mtshan Rinpoche. Also, Kalsang Tenpa Gyaltsen's name appears in the body of this book as bsKal bzang bsTan pa' rGyal mtshan. At a future date, the Mustang Bon Foundation expects to re-issue this book, plus all of the other books using the easier-to-read phonetic spellings, as well as correcting any translation errors that may be found.

May these sacred texts be offered in service to all sentient beings so they may quickly and swiftly achieve complete Buddhahood in this lifetime.

Geshe Sonam Gurung
March 2023, Jomsom, Nepal

Enlightened Intention, The Good Spiritual Life, and Dying into Rainbow Body

Including Translations of The Four Manners of Dying to Accomplish Rainbow Body
&
Blue Lotus Flower
The Sacred Biography of the Venerable Bon Lama, Dawa Dragpa (Zla ba Grags pa)

Enlightened Intention, The Good Spiritual Life, and Dying into Rainbow Body

INTRODUCTION

Enlightened Intention

Kun tu bZang po represents the primordial state of a fully enlightened *Buddha*. In the painting of Kun tu bZang po in consort form, the blue male consort symbolizes the pristine, lucid, bright, limitless expanse of awakened *dharmakāya* space, and the white female consort symbolizes the unobstructed continuous liveliness of awakened awareness.

As a primordial *Buddha*, Kun tu bZang po has a special quality called "enlightened intention" (*dgongs*). Complete *Buddhas* manifest enlightened intention in the form of 1) subduing and taming the mind-streams of immeasurable sentient beings, and 2) guiding sentient beings through various skillful means, and teaching them the spiritual path that guides them out of *saṁsāra* to relocate all sentient beings in awakened *dharmakāya* space.

Enlightened intention is also an inherent quality of the mind-stream of all sentient beings. However, most sentient beings fail to realize that they have enlightened intention because their mind-streams have been clouded over by layers of obscurations and hindrances, and they typically lack sufficient metacognitive awareness to realize their own enlightened intention. However, those ordinary sentient beings that embark on a path of spiritual development, depending on the nature of the path and quality of the teachings, may clear away sufficient obscurations to get a glimpse of enlightened intention operating in their own mind-streams. The more the practitioner clears away obscurations, the more enlightened intention manifests itself in two respects. First, in terms of their spiritual practice and its refinement over time, more and more, the intelligence of the path shows itself to itself, by itself. The spiritual duty of the practitioner is to do the practice diligently, to clear away more and more obscurations, to develop the realization of awakening, stabilize the awakening, self-liberate all residual obscurations until exhausting all negative states of mind and manifesting the flourishing of all positive states of mind (*sangs rgyas*), and stabilizing the experience of full enlightenment. Second, in terms of others, as the practitioner's realization deepens, their spiritual duty more and more emphasizes the manifestation of *bodhicitta* as enlightened activity (*'phrin las*), inexhaustibly subduing the mind-streams of sentient beings and guiding them along the path out of *saṁsāra* to awakened *dharmakāya* space.

Enlightened Activity of a Practitioner During the Dying Process

The manifestation of enlightened intention during the dying process depends on the dying person's level of practice and capacity. Lesser practitioners activate the consciousness-transference (*'pho ba*) practice they had previously learned (typically after completing their hundred thousand preliminary practices) to expand the diameter of the upper central channel, make a hole at the crown, and plug the hole with a seed-syllable. Then, during the dying process they learn to propel the indestructible essence of their condensed individual consciousness from the central channel out the *Brahma* aperture at the crown to relocate it in the expanse of *dharmakāya* as a fully manifest *Buddha*, or if unable to accomplish this, at least guarantee the next rebirth in a manifest pure *Buddha* realm.

Middling practitioners during the dying process are capable of metacognitively remembering the teachings on being guided through the dying process, such as *Training for the Jaws of Death, the Great Staircase of Emancipation* as found in Shar rdza Rinpoche's *sKu gsum rang shar* [*Self-Arising Three-fold Embodiment of Enlightenment*]. These precious teachings give the practitioner voluntary control over the dying process. This middle level practitioner uses the actual dying process intentionally to transfer consciousness to the expanse of *dharmakāya* as a fully enlightened *Buddha*.

A few of the best capacity practitioners have already reached full *Buddhahood* before dying and they are already engaged in the enlightened activity of subduing and guiding sentient beings along the path during this very lifetime. Therefore, the process of dying itself becomes a special occasion for teaching. For example, Geshe Wangyal allowed his students to be with him as he entered the dying process, and used his own experience of the process of dying as a special teaching on the stages of the dying process and recognizing the clear-light of dying.

Introduction

In Great Completion practice, a highly realized master is likely to use the dying process as a teaching on the manifestation of enlightened intention. In order to increase faith and devotion in students and lay people, an extraordinary master will use the dying process itself directly to show how an enlightened mind, even while dying, can have a direct imprint on everyday physical reality in two respects. First, during the dying process, including after physical death, the master continues to practice and dissolves the residual substantiality of the physical body so that within three to seven days the physical body completely disappears, and then manifests as rainbow light floating in space. Rainbow body (*ja lus*) represents the enlightened intention of a great master who, after dying, transforms the dead physical body into rainbow light to inspire faith and devotion in students and non-practitioners alike who witness this miraculous event.

Second, a realized master may not choose to dissolve the physical body into light upon dying and may instead request that the dead body be cremated. When an ordinary person is cremated, the fire consumes everything with respect to the physical body so that only ashes remain. When a realized master is cremated, in addition to the ashes, relics are left behind. Relics are small, typically round, brightly-colored pellets that are seemingly indestructible. Although their composition has not been scientifically analyzed these substances certainly survive the cremation fire. According to the tradition, relics represent the imprint of enlightened intention on physical reality itself. It is said that the greater the level of realization of the master the greater the accumulation of vital "elemental energy" (*dwangs pa*) from the universe during his or her lifetime. When the dead body of such a master is cremated, the vital elemental energy manifests as relics because it is the master's enlightened intention to manifest a miraculous sign directly affecting ordinary physical reality.

Sometimes a great master will manifest enlightened intention in other ways, such as making an imprint on physical reality in the form of a foot or hand print in a stone. For example, at Lubrak in Mustang, Nepal, one of the surviving cave and hermitage Bon yogis, g.Yung drung rGyal mtshan, showed to Dr. Brown and several others a sacred room in his hermitage where several Bon lamas in the past achieved rainbow body.

Outside the hermitage he showed them a rock with the imprint of the foot of one of these yogis, and another rock with the imprint of his yak's hoof.

Rainbow Body and Relics Inspire Faith and Devotion

There is no question that witnessing a rainbow body or seeing sacred relics can inspire faith. In early Christianity, Christ's dead physical body was said to have disappeared after three days in his tomb, then appeared in miraculous ways to his disciples for forty days, and then ascended to heaven.[1] In Christianity the resurrection symbolizes the resurrection of the fully intact physical body at the end of time,[2] and a "triumph of martyrs' bodies over fragmentation, scattering, and the loss of a final resting place."[3]

Francis Tiso, in his book, *Rainbow Body and the Resurrection* (2016), argues that the Christian resurrection and Bon and Buddhist Great Completion rainbow body are very similar. He argues that the Christian resurrection of Christ came first and later was introduced to the Bon and Buddhist Great Completion practitioners through the Syriac Christians who traveled the silk route in the 7th and 8th centuries. Alternatively, it may be that an ancient culture of cave and hermitage yogis existed for several thousand years along what eventually became known as the Silk Route, and that these practices were known by advanced practitioners across multiple religious affiliations or school. While there are no known documents of this resurrection process associated with Christian traditions, it is known that the Tibetans left documents that describe the actual practice of rainbow body.

Within the Tibetan tradition, there are multiple documentations of the practices and teachings on rainbow body; there are known to be three texts that describe four ways of dying in rainbow body practice. The oldest comes from *rNyings ma* Great Completion master, kLong chen

---

1. Tiso, F.T. (2016). *Rainbow Body and the Resurrection*, Berkeley, CA: North Atlantic Books. p. 125.

2. Bynum, C. W. (1995). *The Resurrection of the Body in Western Christianity*, 200-1336. NY: Columbia University Press.

3. Ibid., p. 50.

Introduction

Rab 'byams (1308-1363), in his *Theg pa'i mchog rin po che'i mdzod* [*Treasury of the Supreme Vehicle*]. The next review of the four ways of dying in rainbow body is from the pioneer of the non-sectarian movement, Kong sprul, in his *Shes bya mtha' yas pa'i rgya mtsho* [*Limitless Ocean of What is to be Known*] written about two hundred years ago. The newest is from the Bon Great Completion master Shar rdza bKra' shis rGyal mtshan, as a section in his massive overview of Great Completion, the *dByings rig mdzod* [*The Precious Treasury of the Expanse and Awakened Awareness*] written in the 20th century. All three texts are brief in length and discuss the same four ways of dying in rainbow body practice suggesting that these *rNyings ma* Great Completion, *rKa' rgyud* Mahamudra, and *Bon* Great Completion texts are all drawing from a similar, likely oral transmission source as part of a viable cave and hermitage yogi culture. It is clear that all three schools of Tibetan practice acknowledge the same four ways of dying for the expression of rainbow body.

Rainbow Body as an Event Observed by Others

There are a number of accounts of direct observations by witnesses of rainbow body phenomena. In his book, *Rainbow Body and the Resurrection*, Tiso interviewed attendants, students, and other witnesses of the passing and rainbow body of *rNyings ma* Great Completion master Khen po A Chos. He notes that close to A Chos' death, five-colored rainbows frequently occurred in the sky. As the signs of approaching death became noticeable, the master was placed in sleeping lion posture (laying on his side). According to witnesses, over the next week, the signs of aging of the physical body disappeared and the body appeared more youthful. The physical body progressively became more luminous and the flesh had a distinct luster. Over that week, the physical body emitted a fragrant smell, not the smell of death. Sometimes a soft rain fell that had a fragrant smell, like a rain of flowers. At times over this interval, melodious songs could be heard. Over that week, also, the residual substantiality of the physical body shrunk more and more each day and the physical body got smaller and smaller, until about a week later the physical body disappeared altogether. Typically, the inanimate parts of the body, the hair and nails, remain, but they also disappeared in Khen po A Chos' case.

Once the physical body completely dissolved, the enlightened light body (*'od sku*) manifested close to the site where the physical body dissolved, and also outside in the sky, various sizes and shapes of rainbow light appeared and hovered in space, sometimes for days after the physical body had disappeared.

Namkhai Norbu also presents an account of his uncle, the *rNying ma* Great Completion master Togden Ugyen Tendzin, who achieved rainbow body in 1962. What is especially noteworthy in the account in his book, *Rainbow Body: The Life and Realization of a Tibetan Yogin, Togden Ugyen Tendzin*,[4] is that this full manifestation of rainbow body occurred during the Chinese occupation of Tibet and when Togden Ugyen Tendzin was kept prisoner in a barn guarded by local communist officials. Nevertheless, even these skeptical government officials observed the "dead body sitting upright, the size of a three- or four-year-old child."[5] Sometime later the officials went to inspect the inside of the barn and discovered "that nothing was left except Togden Rinpoche's hair and the nails of his hands and feet."[6]

In rare cases, a body of the master made entirely of light but shaped like a human body will appear in the sky and ascend into the sky until it disappears. The ascension is often accompanied by sweet melodies or chanting and sometimes by a rain of fragrant flowers. An example of this kind of manifestation of the rainbow body of an awareness-holder (*rig 'dzin*) is Garab rDorje (ca. 665 CE), the originator of the *rNyings ma* Great Completion lineage. According to tradition, when he died, his main disciple, Manjushrimitra, fell into despair because he felt that Garab rDorje had died before he received a complete version of the teachings. Therefore, out of a sphere of rainbow light that appeared in the sky, a light body emerged in the form of Garab rDorje, who handed Manjushrimitra a text in a crystal box that contained a precious distillation of all the teachings in three brief essential points, and then disappeared once again.[7]

---

4. Berkeley, CA: North Atlantic Books.

5. Namkhai Norbu, p.52.

6. Ibid., p.54.

7. John Myrdhin Reynolds, *The Golden Letters*. Ithaca NY: Snow Lion, 1996. p. 136.

Introduction

The full manifestation of rainbow body may also be interrupted. In the case of the great Bon master, Shar rdza Rinpoche (1859 – 1934), for example, the process was interrupted. Upon recognizing the signs of dying, Shar rdza Rinpoche explicitly asked his students to place him in a meditation posture and seal him up in a meditation tent for a week. Several days into the process, some of the students became anxious that nothing, not even relics, would be left, so they opened the tent. They observed that Shar rdza Rinpoche's physical body had shrunk to the size of a young child. They broke apart the remaining body to take relics, thereby interrupting the completion of the transition to rainbow body. Shar rdza Rinpoche had previously taught the ways of dying to manifest rainbow body to his main student, Zla ba Grags pa, who manifested a complete rainbow body a year or so earlier.

The Four Ways of Dying to Manifest Rainbow Body

Our main source on the four ways of dying in rainbow body practice is the great *Bon* master Shar rdza bKra shis rGyal mtshan in chapter 19 of his massive work on Great Completion, the *dByings rig mdzod* [*The Precious Treasury of the Expanse and Awakened Awareness*]. Other information comes from the direct observation of witnesses of the complete manifestation of rainbow body by his main student, Zla ba Grags pa, according to Zla ba Grags pa's biographer bsKal bzang bsTan pa' rGyal mtshan. However, as mentioned previously, we have also relied on similar descriptions of the four ways of dying from Kong sprul and kLong chen Rab 'byams.

The manifestation of rainbow body is believed to be available only to the best capacity practitioners. Kong sprul Rinpoche says, "Those yogis of highest capacity, fortunate karmic connection, and diligence, when they reach the final endpoint in this very lifetime, reach the primordial ground of liberation." (4:224) In other words, rainbow body occurs only in those who are of highest capacity, have fortunate karmic connection from lifetimes of previous practice, and who practice diligently before and during the dying process. Such practitioners are likely to see auspicious signs just before dying. Shar rdza Rinpoche says, "At the time when this substantial body and the mind become separated, for those who are not taking a rebirth again but who have fallen, the sign of liberation for them is that they are directly shown *stupas*, relics, sounds, and great visions of light, and then they will reach *Buddhahood*." In the *Tshe dbang snyan rgyud* [*Oral Transmission on Long Life*] it says, "At the time of dying, having auspicious signs of enlightened bodies and root-syllables means they will attain *Buddhahood*." (374) Then the practitioner reads the signs of death, such as changes in the breath, to estimate when the dying process is likely to begin. Then the practitioner assumes a meditation posture. Sometimes, depending on ill health or weakness the practitioner will require assistance to assume an upright meditation posture. A *samādhi* strap is sometimes required to hold the dying body in a good meditation posture. If unable to sit up, the practitioner can assume the sleeping lion posture.

The Manner of Dying Like Space

The first thoroughly cutting through (*khregs chod*) approach to rainbow body is called "the manner of dying like space" (*nam mkha' ltar 'chi lugs*). This practice is a continuation of *dharmadhātu* exhaustion. The practitioner holds the view of the inseparable pair—the view of the limitless expanse of awakened *dharmakāya* space and, simultaneous to that, the view of whatever arises in that expanse as the continuous liveliness of awakened awareness. As part of that view, but not as a strategy, the practitioner lets everything arise and run its own course, without any mental engagement of anything that arises. In this way, whatever arises is immediately liberated leaving no trace, like writing on water and having the form immediately disappear. This meditation is called "self-arising/self-liberated" (*rang snang rang 'grol*). If the practitioner continuously practices holding this view without the slightest mental engagement of anything whatsoever, this forces the mind rapidly and automatically to release all ripening karmic memory traces. Over time as a continuous practice the reservoir of stored karmic memory traces accumulated over lifetimes is gradually exhausted along this path of liberation. Ultimately, the best practitioners reach a state of "purified/flourishing" (*sangs rgyas*) entailing the complete exhaustion of all negative states, including the five poisons, and the flourishing of around eighty positive qualities of a developing *Buddha*-mind.

Introduction

"The manner of dying like space" is an extension and application of the practice of self-arising/self-liberated to the residual substantiality of the physical body during the actual dying process. Thus, this kind of practice is one that the practitioner has likely done for years. With this meditation the residual substantiality of the physical body is reduced to the smallest subtle particles but is not further reduced to pure light. As Shar rdza Rinpoche says, "The way to dissolve having [residual] substantiality of this [physical body] is that through awakened awareness you give up having a physical body as you transfer consciousness, and [the residual substantiality dissolves into the subtlest particles]. This is the manner of 'space-dying'." (374)

At some point, this reduction during the dying process causes the physical body to break apart and seem to disappear. To best describe the dissolution of the physical body, Kong sprul uses the metaphor of breaking apart a clay pot so that the space inside the pot and the space outside the pot are mixed together and become indistinguishable. He says, "Then there are those yogis whose way of dying is like space. When the body-like vase breaks apart and reaches the subtlest particles at the level of original purity, in that timeless [expanse] everything is mixed as the same. What appears as the seeming physical body is much like the space on the inside of the substance [of the vase]. Staying [focused] on the clear-light of the heart, one realizes the original purity inside the physical body. Through shattering the clay substance, the space outside and the space inside become mixed [as the same], such that they are not known as either. One reaches *Buddhahood* not knowing as different 'this is the aggregate wherein the physical body dissolved into the subtlest particles' and 'internal awakened awareness.' This is a sign that you are liberated as transparency at the level of original purity." (4:224) In other words, all that is left is the limitless expanse of *dharmakāya*. The physical body disappears, at least as observable to others. However, the subtlest particles of the physical body remain as liveliness within this expanse. Guinness (2018) adds, "Such a one is already a pure light body…and his or her continued physicality is just a contingent manifestation of one form of enlightened potentiality—in other words it lacks necessity or any inherent reality." (p.207) He adds that this "Atom body is thus not the same as rainbow body, since with the achievement of the former, the body is still *there*, it just can't be seen." (p. 215)

The Manner of Dying Like a Sky-Dancer

Especially in Bon practice, visualizing oneself as inseparable from a powerful *ḍākinī* is an intense skillful means to accomplish certain types of meditation. For example, if the yogi wishes to "balance the elements" in the physical body (*snyom 'jug*), he or she simply visualizes a *ḍākinī* with a skull cup flying around the universe collecting all the elements and vital essences in just the right balance within the skull cup, and then pouring the mix into the crown of the head of the practitioner. Then, the yogi imagines that all the elements in the physical body have become balanced. In a similar manner, the dying practitioner can visualize him or herself as a *ḍākinī* using "intense means" (*bstan thabs*) to rapidly dissolve the residual substantiality of the physical body into the subtlest particles. This method has the advantage of letting the *ḍākinī* do the practice perfectly, especially if the dying practitioner has great physical discomfort or if their mind has been somewhat compromised by the dying process. Shar rdza Rinpoche describes this manner of dying saying, "Similar is [the manner of dying] of the *ḍākinī*s and those miraculously born, who when dying [others] can't see their dead bodies. The manner of dying of a *ḍākinī* is that the physical body is similar to having [lively] awakened awareness, and that the body dissolves into the subtlest particles." (374) As the passage suggests, the intended outcome of this type of thoroughly cutting through practice is also to dissolve the residual substantiality of the physical body into the subtlest particles. Because no one has ever observed a body when a *ḍākinī* dies, likewise, the dissolution of the physical body into the subtlest particles is observed by witnesses as the complete disappearance of the physical body shortly after death. Kong sprul adds that such practitioners, inseparable from the *ḍākinī*, continuously serve the welfare of sentient beings even absent a form body. He says, "There are those much like *ḍākinī*s, who no longer have [after-death states] wherein the signs are bringing the welfare to others through inconceivable emanations in an inconceivable number of worlds." (4:224)[8]

---

8. 4: 224 refers to the fourth volume, page 224.

Both these thoroughly cutting through methods of generating rainbow body, however, do not dissolve these subtlest particles into light. Shar rdza Rinpoche says, "These two ways of [thoroughly cutting through] dying are how thoroughly cutting through liberates into primordial purity, and through that (375) awakened awareness and the expanse become mixed into one, and you don't come back after that." He adds, "The essential point of this is that in the expanse, through purifying the agent of obscuration of its very subtle stains of wind and mind, the internal expanse reaches exhaustion. When you arrive at this level, the materiality of the body dissolves, such that the physical body no longer appears [to self or others]." (375) Kong sprul adds that the residual substantiality of the physical body through the process of *dharmadhātu* exhaustion returns into its 'original purity' (*ka dag*) in the expanse. He says, "[One's] mind dissolves into the *dharmadhātu*, and [everything] is liberation at the level of original purity.... Thus, having gone beyond view and meditation, unhindered by striving for teachings, original purity and spontaneous presence self-appear and through that [complete] liberation naturally arises." (4:224)

The Manner of Dying like a Forest Fire

The main "by-passing" (*thod rgal*) practice is the "lamps" (*sgron ma*) practice of the four levels of visions wherein all of externally appearing substantial reality is transformed into its original purity as light, light-rays, and the ultimate sound of lively awakened awareness. In a related by-passing practice, "inner fire" (*gtum mo*) practice, the residual substantiality of the physical body and residual conceptual thought is purified by central channel inner fire practice. The manner of dying like a forest fire is an extension of by-passing practice in general, and an extension of inner fire practice in particular. The dying practitioner of inner fire locates the indestructible essence of subtle consciousness in the central channel after physical death and then, from that vantage point, resumes central channel practice to ignite the fire using the residuals of the physical body upon dying as the fuel for the fire until all of the residual substantiality of the physical body is rapidly burned away as if being consumed in a massive, rapidly burning forest fire. Shar rdza Rinpoche says, "[First] having dissolved [the residual substantiality of lively] awakened awareness into the expanse, the physical body dissolves into a mass of light. This manner of dying is as a forest fire of flames." (374) Kong sprul adds that this advanced practice is for those yogis who have reached the very endpoint of meditation practice in this lifetime prior to dying. He says, "There are those yogis for whom the way they die reflects that they have reached the very endpoint of meditation practice, as an example, by having exhausted the firewood [the body] as the cause [or basis of a] a great mass of fire, the fire dies, as if the fire has exhausted itself." (4:224) In this approach all of the elements that constitute the aggregates of the physical body are consumed, along with any residual imprints of afflictive emotions, conceptual thoughts, and karmic memory traces that might remain throughout the dying process. He adds, "By exhausting the cause of the elements and the conditions, the substantiality of the aggregates becomes insubstantial. The signs are such that the afflictive emotions are liberated in their own place." (4:224)

The Manner of Dying like an Awareness-Holder

The second by-passing method for achieving the full manifestation of rainbow body during the dying process is called "the manner of dying like an awareness-holder" (*rig 'dzin*). This manner of manifesting rainbow body is the most spectacular and miraculous from the perspective of witnesses. In this approach, the very advanced practitioner is already fully enlightened prior to dying and is therefore capable of emanating at will in any seeming form he or she wishes as an expression of the full measure of enlightened intention. This type of rainbow body practitioner upon dying appears not just as rainbow lights in the sky, but more specifically as an enlightened form-body of light (*'od sku*), i.e., a body made purely of light but in the shape of his or her original physical body. In a miraculous display, that light body ascends in the sky in front of disciples, students, and lay witnesses, and the ascension is often accompanied by melodious music or chanting, and by a rain shower of fragrant flowers made of light.[9] Kong sprul emphasizes the miraculous display

---

9. Using kLong chen pa as a source, Matthew Kapstein (2004) adds that an awareness-holder "may vanish in the sight of the public in the midst of a mass of light and ac-

Introduction

of this approach to rainbow body saying, "As for the signs of this, when [the awareness-holders] ascend up [in the sky] they seem to have the aggregate of the physical body, and there are sounds and lights in the sky seen by everyone." (4:224) Shar rdza Rinpoche describes the manner of the awareness-holders saying, "[The other way of dying in by-passing] is the way of awakened awareness-holders, whose [bodies of] light and [miraculous] sounds [ascend] in the sky and then disappear." (375) In this approach, no method is needed because the rainbow body is already spontaneously present as an aspect of the full measure of enlightenment prior to the dying process. All that is required to produce the miraculous display is the enlightened intention to emanate to serve the welfare of the witnesses of this ascension and an enlightened light body. As Shar rdza adds, "In by-passing, [the residuals of the physical body] are liberated as spontaneously present." (375)

In by-passing, as compared to thoroughly cutting through practice, even the subtlest particles of the residual substantiality of the physical body dissolve completely into light. In all four manners of dying as rainbow body, the residual substantiality of the physical body dissolves sufficiently so that the physical body seems to observers to have completely disappeared and manifests as rainbow light. In this sense, all four methods are similar. As Kong sprul says, "By [the residuals] dissolving in the domain of space of spontaneous presence and original purity, you therefore become liberated. While practicing accordingly [with thoroughly cutting and by-passing] in stages, even though there are distinct capacities, the fruition of each of these has the very same essence as its secret interior landscape of precious *dharmakāya*." (4:224)

John Reynolds makes an interesting distinction between these types of rainbow body methods in *The Golden Letters* (1996). He says that the kind of rainbow body attained in thoroughly cutting through practice using the space of sky-dancer methods is technically referred to as "rainbow body" (*'ja lus*) because the residual substantiality of the physical body dissolves into the subtlest particles. He says that the kind of rainbow body attained through by-passing practice is technically referred to

---

companied by sounds and lights…when they ascend to even higher planes, do so bodily, going into the sky with sounds and lights that are visible to all." (p. 144)

as "the enlightened body of light" (*'od sku*) because on this occasion these subtlest particles dissolve into pure light. A third kind of rainbow body practice is reserved for the awareness-holders. This is called "the great consciousness transference" (*'pho ba chen po*).

The Dying Practitioner's Enlightened Intention Manifesting as an Imprint on Ordinary Physical Reality as Bones and Relics

According to tradition, when the body of an enlightened master is cremated, in addition to what is normally expected, namely that the physical body is reduced entirely to ash, among the ashes there are small round brightly colored pellets that seem indestructible by fire. The greater the strength of the master's realizations, the more "pure elemental radiance" from these realizations accumulates in the body such that when the physical body is destroyed by cremation these relics appear among the ash. Shar rdza Rinpoche explains, "The relics are similar to the bones. The shape is similar to the bones but they could be any of the five colors. The cause is pure elemental radiance, having purified the white and red *bodhicitta* substance, the flesh and bones, the warmth and breath, and condensed them into the elemental radiance. The bones originate from the most pure elemental radiance. The distinction between the bones and relics is such that bones can't be destroyed by the elements by putting them into a mortar and pestle and pulverizing them; (12-378) and the relics are such that they can't be destroyed by anything [so] if you put relics into the ashes [of a fire] they won't burn. If these relics become manifest after a Great Completion yogi dies, it is a sign that he gave up his last breath in the *Buddha*-fields of the natural Manifest Emanating *Buddha*-fields. The others are uncertain." (12-377-378) According to Shar rdza Rinpoche, even ordinary people at certain times and situations manifest relics, but these normally do not emanate light, nor are they accompanied by special signs. He says, "Even ordinary people, birds, dogs, corrupt people, and highly educated lamas with their speculation have relics. Some will be born in a higher realm, and some will be born in a lower realm. The relics of ordinary people and *Buddhas* are different in terms of whether they have the signs of total elemental radiance or not, whether they have clear-light or not, and whether they have the signs with the Bodhi tree and the milk of this." (378)

Enlightened Intention Manifest in This Very Lifetime; the Good Spiritual Life

The greater the level of realization of a practitioner, the more practice shifts from accumulating further meditation experiences and personal realizations to conduct that inexhaustibly serves the welfare of others. In the Tibetan Bon and Buddhist traditions, the authenticity of spiritual realization is necessarily measured by conduct. Genuine masters live a life that leaves a wake of positive influence around them—a life that single-mindedly serves the greater social good.

Therefore, another way to explore how enlightened intention manifests is to look at the life course of great masters, who not only manifest rainbow body or relics when they die, but also live a life of greatness while alive. In this sense, a very good way to understand the manifestations of enlightened intention in everyday life is to study sacred biographies.

Blue Lotus Flower – Sacred Biography of Zla ba Grags pa

His Holiness the 33rd Menri Trizin, the lineage holder of the Bon, strongly recommended that we translate the sacred biography of the great master Shar rdza Rinpoche's main student, Zla ba Grags pa. He said that this biography contained a detailed experiential description of rainbow body practice and its observation by others. What His Holiness didn't say, but left us to discover, is that this sacred biography is exemplary of the good life worth living. It is an example of the life of a practitioner who studied hard with a great teacher; mastered the three main Bon traditions of Great Completion practices, as well as approach and accomplishment stages of tantric visualizations, both through study and extensive retreat; expressed his level of realizations through spontaneous songs of realization; showed clear signs of accomplishment of his realizations; single-mindedly served the welfare of many beings through teaching and service; and in the process of dying manifested rainbow body in a manner like a forest fire. As an example of rainbow body practice specifically, but also generally about how enlightened intention continuously manifests throughout the life of a great practitioner, this book offers a complete translation of the sacred biography of Zla ba Grags pa as exemplary of the best spiritual practice, and of leading the good spiritual life.

Enlightened Intention, The Good Spiritual Life, and Dying into Rainbow Body

Including Translations of The Four Manners of Dying to Accomplish Rainbow Body
&
Blue Lotus Flower
The Sacred Biography of the Venerable Bon Lama, Dawa Dragpa
(Zla ba Grags pa)

the successor to the incomparable
Shardza Tashi Gyaltsen Rinpoche
(Shar rDza bKra' shis rGyal mtshan Rinpoche)

Written By
Kalsang Tenpa Gyaltsen
(bsKal bzang bsTan pa' rGyal mtshan)

Enlightened Intention, The Good Spiritual Life, and Dying into Rainbow Body

PART II

TRANSLATIONS OF THE FOUR MANNERS OF DYING IN RAINBOW BODY PRACTICE

A. A selected passage from Shar rdza Rinpoche's *dByings rig mdzod* [*The Precious Treasury of the Expanse and Awakened Awareness*]:

19.2.2 **The signs of liberation in the *after-death bardos* or thereafter** 12-373

Second, the explanation of the signs of liberation in the *bardo* or thereafter has two parts: 1) A brief explanation; and 2) An extensive explanation.

19.2.2.1 **Brief explanation** 12-373

First: even though you have entered into the path of Great Completion, if your [level] of diligence is low, the full measure of liberation doesn't come. At the time when this substantial body and the mind become separated, for those who are not taking a rebirth again but who have fallen, the sign of liberation for them is that they are directly shown *stupas*, relics, sounds, and great visions of light, and then they will reach *Buddhahood*. In the *Tshe dbang snyan rgyud* [*Oral Transmission on Long Life*] it says, "At the time of dying, having auspicious signs of enlightened bodies and root-syllables means they will attain *Buddhahood*." (12-374)

Furthermore, the manner of achieving what is called "completing *Buddhahood*" has two parts. In the *mGo'i zhva lta bu'i gdams* [*Instructions Like a Hat*] it says, "This is directly completing *Buddhahood*. This is the genuine completion of *Buddhahood*." With respect to this, if we were to categorize the manner of realization, the former is *Buddha* sTon pa gShen rab Me po and includes any person [after that] for whom the realization has arisen. The latter is the first to take the throne of Kun tu bZang po [after that].

Furthermore, if we were to categorize the manner of liberation, the former pertains to some [who become enlightened and] have remaining substantiality, but have enlightened bodies, seed-syllables, sound, and immeasurable visions of light, and through that directly attain *Buddhahood*. The latter pertains to those with the best diligence, for whom having a substantial body has dissolved [into light] so that they are without any physical body remaining, and they complete genuine *Buddhahood*.

(1) The way to dissolve having substantiality of this [physical body] is by awakened awareness having a physical body it vanishes into subtle particles that scatter in the manner of "space-dying;" and it is somewhat like the *ḍākinīs* and those miraculously born who, when dying, you can't see their dead bodies.

(2) The manner of dying of a *ḍākinī* is that within the body they have awakened awareness and that body dissolves into subtle particles. These are the two ways of dying [in thoroughly cutting through practice]. Primordial purity liberates in thoroughly cutting practice, and through that (12-375) awakened awareness and the expanse become mixed into one, and you don't come back after that.

Furthermore, there are two [by-passing] ways of dying:

(3) Having dissolved awakened awareness into the expanse, the physical body dissolves into a mass of light. This manner of dying is as a forest fire of flames.

(4) [The other way of dying] is the way of awakened awareness-holders, wherein with holding awakened awareness [in a stable way] and accompanied by the [melodious] sounds of space, [the physical body completely] dissolves into light.

This is the spontaneous liberation in by-passing. The essential point of this is that, in the expanse, through purifying the agent of obscuration of its very subtle stains of wind and mind, the internal expanse reaches exhaustion. When you arrive at this level, the materiality of the body dissolves, such that the physical body no longer appears.

19.2.2.2 **Extended explanation** 12-375

Second, the extended explanation has five parts:

(1) Light;

(2) Bones;

(3) Sound;

(4) Earth-shaking; and

(5) Enlightened body.

19.2.2.2.1 **Light** 12-375

The first has four parts:

(1) Essence;

(2) Cause;

(3) Categories; and

(4) The certainty of the full measure of liberation.

19.2.2.2.1.1 **Essence** 12-375

The essence is that the elemental self-radiance of awakened awareness is the self-clarity of the five colored lights.

19.2.2.2.1.2 **Cause** 12-375

The cause is gathering both practicing in the five lights and gathering the elements into elemental radiance. This is in accordance with both the *rTags tshad sgron ma* [*Lamp of the Full Measure of Signs*] and the *gSer gyi yang* [*(Very) Refined Gold*] where it says, "Oh! Children of the lineage! This is the full measure of the external [signs]. The full measure of light is the visions of light."

19.2.2.2.1.3 **Categories** 12-375

The categories are the three: going upward; rotating on the periphery; and like ribs [drawn on] a wall.

19.2.2.2.1.4 **The certainty of the full measure of liberation** 12-375

The certainty of the full measure of liberation pertains to the signs of liberation in the first *bardo* from the primordial pure visions, namely either as if [there are] spokes of light being pulled upwards, or appearing as if rotating. (12-376) Furthermore, if [the sign is such that] it occurs like ribs, that is when liberation will come in the last *bardo* [of becoming].

19.2.2.2.2 **Bones** 12-376

Second, bones are described in the *Tshe dbang snyan rgyud* [*Oral Transmission on Long Life*] where it says, "There are five: 1. *Sha ri ram*; 2. *Chu ri ram*; 3. *Pan cha ram*; 4. *Nya ri ram*; and 5. *Ba ri ram*." Also, according to this saying, there are two—bones and relics.

There are five bones—*sha ri ram* and so forth. With respect to these five bones, each comes with a particular color and from a particular cause, either peaceful or wrathful. The colors of the peaceful bones are: *sha ri ram*, white; *ba ri ram*, blue; *chu ri ram*, yellow; *pan cha ram*, red; and *nya ri ram*, green. The color of the wrathful bones are: *sha ri ram*, white; *ba ri ram*, yellow; *chu ri ram*, blue; *nya ri ram*, brown; and *pan cha ram*, dark green. Furthermore, the four peaceful bones are *shar ri ram, ba ri ram, chu ri ram and bse ri ram*, respectively occurring from the bones, warmth, blood, and the elemental radiance of the elements. *Nya ri ram* is what occurs from gathering the mind into [its essence of] elemental radiance without remainder. The five wrathful bones are *sha ri ram, chu ri ram, ba ri ram, nya ri ram*, and *pan cha ram*. The cause of each of these is from the skull [derived] from the view, from the blood, from the joints, and from the feet occurring from the elemental radiance of the elements. (12-377) The location of *sha ri ram* is the head; of *ba ri ram* is the first rib; *chu ri ram* the liver; *bse ri ram* is from the kidney; and of *nya ri ram* is the top of the lungs. The size of *sha ri ram* is similar to the size of a white chickpea. The others are about the size of a white mustard seed or a small pea. The shape of all five bones is spherical like a ball. They are translucent inside and when shown to the sun's rays they are shiny and bright. These bones are from practice that purified the energy drops of awakened awareness's elemental radiance. In the *rTags sgron ma che ba* [*Great Lamp of Signs*] it says, "The best size of the bones is about the size of energy drops." The origin of the peaceful bones is from where there are the signs of certainty of understanding at a level liberated as self-appearance. The origin of the wrathful bones begins with the signs of having achieved the five enlightened bodies.

The relics are similar to the bones. The shape is similar to the bones, but they could be any of the five colors. The cause is pure elemental radiance, having purified the white and red *bodhicitta* substance, the flesh and bones, the warmth and breath, and condensed them into the elemental radiance. The bones originate from the most pure elemental radiance. The distinction between the bones and relics is such that bones can't be destroyed by the elements except by putting them into a mortar and pestle and pulverizing them, (12-378) and the relics are such that they can't be destroyed by those, but [also] if you put relics into the ashes [of a fire] they won't burn. If these relics [occur] to a Great Completion yogi, that is a sign that he gave up his last breath in the *Buddha*-fields of the Natural Manifest Emanating *Buddha*-field.

The others are uncertain. Even ordinary people, birds, dogs, corrupt people, and highly educated lamas with their speculation, [can] have relics. Some will be born in a higher realm, and some will be born in a lower realm. The relics of ordinary people and *Buddhas* are different in terms of whether they have the signs of total elemental radiance or not, whether they have clear-light or not, and whether they have the signs with the Bodhi tree and the milk of this.

B. Kong sprul's description of the four manners of dying in rainbow body practice from the *Shes bya mrtha' yas pa'i rgya mtsho* [*Limitless Ocean of What is to Be Known*]:

Those of highest capacity dissolve [the residual substantiality of the physical body] at the level of primordial exhaustion [in one of four ways]—like a *ḍākinī*, like an awareness-holder, like a mass of fire, and like space.

All these, however, are the same within the precious secret interior landscape.

Those yogis of highest capacity, fortunate karmic connection, and diligence, when they reach the final endpoint in this very lifetime, reach the primordial ground of liberation.

There are those, much like *ḍākinī*s, who no longer have [after-death states], and where the signs are their bringing the welfare to others through inconceivable emanations in an inconceivable number of worlds. There are those yogis for whom the way they die shows they have reached the very endpoint of meditation practice. For example, through having exhausted the firewood [of the body] as the cause [of the fire,] after a great mass of fire, and through it, it dies, as if the fire had exhausted itself.

By exhausting the cause of the elements and the conditions, the substantiality of the aggregates becomes insubstantial. The signs are such that the afflictive emotions are liberated in their own place.

Then there are those yogis whose way of dying is like space. When the vase-like body breaks apart and reaches the subtlest particles at the level of original purity, in that timeless [expanse] everything is mixed as the same. What appears as the seeming physical body is much like the space on the inside of the substance [of the vase]. Staying [focused] on the clear-light of the heart, one realizes the original purity inside the physical body. Through shattering the clay substance, the space outside and the space inside become mixed [as the same], such that they are not known as either. One reaches *Buddhahood* not knowing as different "this is the aggregate wherein the physical body dissolved into the subtlest particles" and "internal awakened awareness." This is a sign that you are liberated as transparency at the level of original purity.

The first and last pertain to cutting through. The two in between pertain to by-passing or surpassing the cycle of the great secret for reaching the end of the path. Through thoroughly cutting through, the physical body dissolves into the subtlest particles, one's mind dissolves into the *dharmadhātu*, and [everything] is liberated at the level of original purity. Through by-passing, even the subtlest particles dissolve and [become] clear-light, and you gain mastery over rebirth. You attain the cycle of great consciousness transference, and, surpassing [everything], you serve the welfare of sentient beings.

Thus, having gone beyond view and meditation, unhindered by striving for teachings, original purity and spontaneous presence self-appear, and through that [complete] liberation naturally arises. By [the residuals] dissolving in the domain of space of spontaneous presence and original purity, you therefore become liberated. While practicing accordingly [with thoroughly cutting and by-passing] in stages, even though there are distinct capacities, the fruition of each of these has the very same essence as its secret interior landscape of precious *dharmakāya*. This is similar to different containers [dissolving] into the same expanse of space, or different rivers becoming one and the same within a great ocean.

Enlightened Intention, The Good Spiritual Life, and Dying into Rainbow Body

PART III

BLUE LOTUS FLOWER –
THE SACRED BIOGRAPHY OF DAWA DRAGPA
(ZLA BA GRAGS PA)

[WHOSE SPIRITUAL NAME IS KUNZANG NAMKHI NYINGPO (KUN BZANG NAM MKHA' SNYING PO)]

(599) This is the extraordinary biography called the "blue lotus flower" of the venerable lama, who [achieved the] great rainbow body, the son of dBra, [Zla ba Grags pa, Chandrakirti], whose [spiritual] name was Kun bzang Nam mkha' sNying po [meaning Kun bzang-space-essence]. (600) I pay homage with respect to the glorious Lord, primordial Kun [tu] bZang [po], whose [enlightened mind] is inseparable from the venerable holy lama. (601) He had attained the *enlightened intention* of Kun tu bZang po in the primordial expanse and saw the visions of the pure lands of the *sambhogakāya* in the space of primordial wisdom. The supreme one, who is the holder of the teachings, [embodies] the *essence* of the skillful means to subdue [the mind-streams of sentient beings]. I pay homage to the feet of this venerable lama. [He came] from a place in the pure god-realms to this human world. He made these teachings of the unsurpassed vehicle of the *sutras* and *tantras* flourish by teaching them individually to children of the lineage. I pay homage to the lineage and teachers of the threefold embodiment of enlightenment.[1] They hold the unbroken lineage of these three unsurpassed lineages, and the twenty-four [previous Bon masters] who attained the great consciousness-transference of rainbow body, and the father and the immortal sons of [the father] Dran pa Nam mkha', namely the sons Tshe dbang Rig 'dzin, Pad ma [mThong

---

1. The teachings of the *sutras* are associated with *nirmāṇakāya* and Khri gtsugs rGyal ba; the *tantras* are associated with the *sambhogakāya* and gShen lha 'Od dkar; and the unsurpassed Great Completion is associated with the *dharmakāya* and Kuntu bzang po.

grol], and mNyam med [Shes rab rGyal mtshan]. I give reverence and faith to all the holders of the teachings of Zhang Zhung and Tibet. I generate unequalled *bodhicitta* by relying on this chariot. (602) It brought the daylight to all those practitioners of the unsurpassed vehicle of Great Completion. It has served as a guide to those followers during degenerate times and brought them to the expanse. I give praise to all those disciples who follow the teachings of Shar rdza [Rinpoche]. Even during this degenerate age, this unsurpassed [vehicle] makes the path clear.

This is the biography of one who had directly achieved rainbow body, which is similar to the [rare] *audumvara* flower. This is the amazing ornament of the beauty of the appearance of the doctrine of [sTon pa] g.Shen rab. His three— [external, internal] and secret positive qualities—extend throughout space. Even the great flapping wings of a powerful *garuda* cannot tell where the edge of space is. How can those who are less intelligent like me ever tell [his full story]? However, having generated in my mind some familiarity with his life story, may this serve to generate faith in others of fortunate karmic connections. For that reason, from the knowledge of this venerable lama that is like an immense ocean, I will write a few drops of water to nurture the faithful. Then, in the primordial expanse, by the gift-waves of influence of Kun tu bZang po and gShen lha 'Od dkar, the teachers of self-appearing great compassion in the 'Og Min pure realm taught limitless teachings of the unsurpassed Bon vehicle. The supplements to those teachings are the doctrines of the *tantra* and *sutra* paths. By the various ways of transmission, these [teachings] spread from very early times in this world. In these degenerate times, through the compassion generated by the teachers of the three-fold embodiment of enlightenment, the doctrines of the *sutras*, *tantras* and unsurpassed [Great Completion] vehicles (603) have proliferated throughout the human world. In a very short time his [sTon pa g.Shen rab's] enlightened mind-teachings[2] [spread throughout] this world. In both Zhang Zhung and Tibet, there have been the oral transmission of the unsurpassed vehicle and the *bKa' brgyud skor bzhi* [*Four*

---

2. When sTon pa gShen rab was alive, he presented the teachings in an enlightened body. After he passed away, his successor conveyed his precious enlightened heart teachings, but those teachings have degenerated over time. Eventually what was left was only what was written, namely his enlightened speech teachings.

Cycles of the Authoritative Lineage] instructions. Through these instructions alone twenty-four [previous Bon] masters came [into this world and left], who had achieved the great consciousness-transference of rainbow body, and there have been additional immeasurable beings who have gone beyond even the smallest particles [of the residual physical body] with nothing remaining. Out of these, right now in this moment, relying on the definitive knowledge of the three instructions—*A Khrid*, Great Completion, and the oral transmission[3]—directly leads to achieving the result, namely that the solidness [of the physical body] dissolves into light. The yogi who has this definitive knowledge is a *Mahāsiddha* of the great rainbow body. If we had to say his name for some reason, his name would be dBra sras Zla ba Grags pa or, [his spiritual name], Kun bzang Nam mkha' sNying po. This great master, a lama who is very famous in this world, came into it [this world] like an *audumvara* flower. I can't exactly tell his entire biography, which would be the secret and profound story of his enlightened body, speech, and mind. However, right now, with [the help of] those to be subdued [followers of him], who have seen or heard about him, that is just how my mind was able to evaluate him, [in a way that] had not been corrupted by false speech. For those of the fortunate ones who are his followers, I am happy to briefly tell [this story] about him.

1.0 His Early Life

I will summarize the periods of his life: what was his past life; when he took birth; how he entered into spiritual life (604); his maturation, liberation, and meditation experiences; his achievement of the profound treasure with the signs of the path; his deeds for the teachings and for the purpose of sentient beings; how he joined the lineage practice; and in the end, how he achieved rainbow body. These are the topics upon which I will speak to tell this extraordinary story.

1.1 His Previous Lifetimes

Furthermore, if we were to talk about the basis of the great venerable

---

3. These refer to the three lineages of Bon Great Completion—*A Khrid, yang rtse* [*Epitome*], and the *Zhang Zhung nyan rgyud* [*Oral Transmission from Zhang Zhung*].

one's previous lives, having directly manifested the enlightened intention of the primordial original purity, he [must] have mastered the status of the three-fold embodiment of enlightenment, and because of that we can say [in his past life] he was some kind of *Buddha*. There is no dispute. We can't recognize him for certain as exactly this or that [*Buddha*], but from the mouth of the great emanation and treasure discoverer, Gar dbang Sang sngags gLing pa, [he says our venerable one is associated with] gSang ba 'Dus pa, the principal of all the *Buddha* families, as an aspect of appearance as the play of the primordial wisdom of the *sambhogakāya* deity Kun sngang Khyab pa, the great sovereign lord of all the complete teachings of the *tantras*. The venerable deity gSang ba'i bDag po gSang 'Dus pa is the very basis of [this life's current] emanation as the venerable Zla ba Grags pa.

This is the very essence of the enlightened heart-mind of all the victorious *Buddhas*, and the *Buddhas* and *bodhisattva*s in all the realms of *saṁsāra* and *nirvāṇa*, wherein everything is displayed as this play. Having relied on that, he holds all the secret treasures of the *Buddhas*. He has engaged in unhindered enlightened *Mahāsiddha* activities everywhere in this world for the teachings and vastly for serving the purpose of sentient beings, in all directions and at all times (605) without limitation. After that, in these [current] times [associated with] the founder, the omniscient Ston pa gShen rab's doctrine, he emanated as g.Yung drung gTsug gshen rGyal ba in the land of sTag gzig. There he served the welfare of sentient beings and [spread the] teachings. At that time, he became the heart-son of our founder sTon pa [gShen rab]. He attained mastery of the power of retention and [mind] training. Through that he could teach any kind of teaching and hold everything. Having relied upon the three baskets of teachings and the three-fold training for realization, he became the successor of the remaining followers of the founder, sTon pa gShen rab. Through the tones of his enlightened speech, and his pure conduct he was praised by and trusted by all the kings, sages, and so forth. After that, in the location of Zhang Zhung and Tibet when spreading the teachings by the thirteen family lineages, he emanated as the Bon master [and great magician] Zin pa mThu chen to protect his followers. After that, in China, at a location known as Gang bud mar ru, using the *sPhyi spungs* *skor gsum* [*The Three Cycles of the Collection of Tantras*], he attained mastery of the generation-stages, and also perfected the yoga of the completion-stages, and through that he attained the marks of having mastered magical display and the four elements. Through that the teachings on the essence of the secret mind spread throughout the countries of China, Tibet, and Zhang Zhung, and he developed the power of enlightened activity. (606)

Thus, he had limitless displays of emanations. However, I haven't seen the text [describing] his reincarnations, so I wasn't able to write everything about [those reincarnations], let alone [identify] the names of the people who were his great [previous] reincarnations, or [specify] how many [rebirths are] included in all his rebirths. By relying on what I could, I tried to write just what is here, after having endeavored to generate definite understanding and trust in my mind.

In the expanse of original purity of all the *Buddhas* of the three times, which is like undivided space that has many reflections from the same moon, this display of limitless emanations is inconceivable. In the place of the three roots [the deity] gSang ba 'Dus pa [emanated as] g.Yung drung gTsug gShen rGyal ba at the location of sTag gZigs. In Zhang Zhung, Tibet, and China [he also emanated] as Zing pa mThu chen. Saying or writing your name, [Zla ba Grags pa], is melodious. You are the person who holds the treasure of all the positive qualities of the two accomplishments. How amazing is this feat of reincarnation! Aren't all the positive qualities of the three secrets [body, speech, and mind] of the spiritual guides accomplished all at once by you, oh, sacred one?

1.2 His Birth

From this current time [in history], in our visions [we saw] how this venerable holy lama was to be born. If you were to ask in what place he was born, it was the best place to which the precious *Buddha* teachings had spread. (607) In the Yar Lung dynasty in eastern Tibet, in Khams, near the long mountain range of brDa sgang, is a monastic center of the second *Buddha*, the venerable great master Shar rdza [bKra' shis rGyal mtshan]. It is [located] at a holy site in Khams called Gyer za g.yung drung lhun po, on the left [side of the mountain] at a well-known place.

[The monastic center] located there is called dPal gyi sTeng chen gShen bstan mdo sngags g.Yung drung bStan rgyas gLing. It is in a town called lCang mNgon. This place, from the beginning, was a special place where there was a field of influence of the magic of Bon. Therefore, up until now innumerable holy beings, [such as] dBra ston Chen po Blos gros Ring mo and others were born there. It is the region where all the Bon teachings, all the positive qualities, and the wealth of existence without remainder were gathered from all directions and spread there.

From what family lineage was he born? It is in the mDo Kham region in northern Khams. Out of three well-known families—the dBra, lCang, and sMon—from these great descendants of the lineage holders of the Bon, the teachings would never vanish. Out of them come the descendants of a family lineage called Sa skyongs dBra. There are many ways to describe how family lineages spread [the teachings], but this family lineage, coming from the region of Shar rdza, really established the Bon teachings there. Those lamas, endowed with being learned and well-practiced, did great deeds regarding the [Bon] teachings. Over time, the monastic center was taken care of by the succession of lamas. Right now (608) from the family lineage of Lwa shu gyi Rus las, came the great dBra family reincarnation, [namely the venerable lama's father], bsTan 'dzin dBang rgyal. The immortal Dran pa Nam mkha' directly gave the gift-waves of influence to this great *Mahāsiddha*, who mixed as inseparable appearance and mind, and who was very famous (like the wind being everywhere) to both those educated and illiterate.

The [venerable lama's] mother's name is bDe skyid lCam. She came from the family lineage of A chen Hor. Her lineage is free from the faults of common girls and women because it is endowed with the great signs of the primordial wisdom *ḍākinī*. He [the venerable lama] had the enlightened intention to be born as the son of those two [parents]. He entered [his mother's] womb already having paranormal abilities. From that point in time, his mother's physical condition became healthier and lighter. Great meditation experience of non-conceptual stillness arose in her enlightened mind. Many young girls prayed and paid respect to her, and she had a sign in her dreams of having the retinue of [the *ḍākinīs*], dBu med Nag po and dre'u Mar Mo, and so forth. It was said that she had signs of *ḍākinī*s gathering around her and being surrounded by these protectors.

Then, during a complete cycle that the Indians call the *rtsi tra*, he was born during the 15th year of a sixty-year cycle. Tibetans have many ways of describing this [cycle]. In Chinese it is called *bzhin lwu*. In the area where he was destined to be born, he was born during the new year of the female water-horse. When he was born, his head was spherical like an umbrella, and his crown protruded. He was already adorned with the signs of a holy person. (609) He was like nectar in the eyes of every sentient being. Amazing signs [occurred when he was born]. There was no harm whatsoever to his mother [during child birth]. He was born like the moon rising above a mountain in the east.

There were two brothers. It says that he was the eldest. At that time [of his birth], the father, a Rinpoche, recognized his infant as the incarnation of the master of meditation experience and realization, dBra dBon, bsTan 'dzin mChog legs, and [knew that] in the future he was [destined] to become a yogi with mastery over mind and appearance. He prophesized this directly, namely that [his son] would have direct amazing signs within himself of paranormal abilities, like knowing what would happen in the future.

The way he awakened to his potential during his childhood will now be discussed. Right after he was born he recited, "*A*," and, "*HUNG*." At the time he was between three and four years old there was nothing about his manner that looked like an [ordinary] child. Instead of playing, he drew letters on the wall. He gave initiations to his childhood friends and preached the teachings. Many times it seemed as if he remained in concentrative-evenness. Quite often he said, "I am a lama," and "I have to go to an isolated mountain hermitage." He had habitual karmic tendencies [indicating] that [likely] many times he had been reborn again and again as a holy person, (610) as if the form of [being reborn as a holy person] was never modified but kept automatically repeating itself. This is [a story] unlike some other elder Tibetans who are deceitful, and who purposely modify [the story of their children] as if they were a reincarnation [of a holy person], but [one who is] entirely fake. Therefore, all those people near to him understood that he was not an ordinary person. They said that this must be a holy person. That brought faith to their minds, and also joy and happiness.

Adorned with the glory of all good things and wealth, in the place where billions of teachings of the *sutras* and *tantras* spread, he was held [dearly] by many noble and exalted people. It is completely clear that in the area called Shar rdza, he came to the lord of the dBra family, an actual appearance of immortal gYer spungs [Dran pa Nam mkha']. He came directly into a family lineage of the *Mahāsiddhas*. This child was adorned with many extraordinary favorable signs. His enlightened form-body was to blossom with a face like the moon, and to have all the major and minor marks [of a holy person]. Right after he was born, he gave up all the [normal] ways of his childhood, and he [acted like] a holy being. He awakened to his potential with all kinds of favorable signs. It is certain that his familiarity [as a holy person] came from many, many lifetimes.

1.3 How He Entered the Spiritual Life

[Now I will discuss] how he entered into the gateway of the teachings, starting from his early home-life to when he became a monk. At around seven years of age, he disliked the activities and customs of ordinary homes (611) and had become much happier being around lamas and monks. [Toward them] he developed extraordinary interest and faith from the depths of his heart. His holy father, dBra sprul Rinpoche bsTan 'dzin dBang rgyal, said that when his son came as a reincarnated lama it reminded him that he also was a reincarnated lama. When both such favorable conditions had co-emerged and came together, right away his father [cut a tuft of hair] from his son's crown and offered it. After that his father gave him refuge vows and the name Zla ba Grags pa. Thereafter, up until the current time, his name has become very famous.

After that, he trained in the way of learning from the treasure of the heart. He relied on his teacher, who was very famous. His teacher had his own meditation experiences and realizations. He was a monk whose body was adorned with monk's clothing. He was also a high lama. He was called bDe dga'. By studying to get a foundation in education, writing and reading, he learned very well without taking very long. He also [studied other subjects], such as divination, astrology, and so forth, and mostly Tibetan science, which he studied a little bit with other [teachers]. He was very skilled in learning and in understanding.

Having relied on his teacher, who was named slob dpon Lha Kho, he studied music, dance, the *mandala*, the process of the ritual of the five deities of the father *tantras*, gSas mkhar mchog, and also the traditions of their own regions. (612) When studying he learned very well from a lama named bSam gtan Ye shes, who had studied at the highest monastic institute at sMan ri [Monastery], and also from the second highest [g.Yung drung gLing] there, both of whom followed the Bru family tradition, as to how to make the *mandalas* and the process of the rituals. From others also he learned the process of the rituals, the *mudrās*, and the masked dance of the gShen family tradition.

At that time, those teachers gave him teachings from inside the texts, namely the extensive teachings of the Great Completion lineage, the practical guides, and so forth, of which there are so many. In between [the actual teaching sessions] he read these and understood their meaning and words. At that time, he was still young, and he didn't study that much. However, in his heart great faith had been born, so he thought he should practice well, and generate interest about them again and again. I heard from his disciples that he was like that [when he studied]. Similarly, he had the signs of the fruition of sustaining practice on the higher vehicle in his previous lives. In this life he [also showed signs that] ripened into the [full] fruition or outcome from [what had started in] these previous lives. We don't need to mention that these refer to special signs of ripening.

One time in his childhood he went with his father to central Tibet for a pilgrimage. (613) Because of having faith and admiration co-emergent in his mind-stream, he made a deep connection [on the way] with lamas and the sacred sites. [At one point] they arrived at a mountain called Bon ri in the region of rKong po. There he circumambulated the mountain Bon ri one time with full prostrations. Then, he circumambulated [another] ten times. He purified the obscurations of body and speech. He never saw virtuous activities as being difficult. He worked hard and was very diligent. At that time [in his childhood], people familiar with him said that he didn't engage in activities much differently than most others, but whatever he did, he did in a solitary way. Most of the time everybody said he had single-minded pursuit of the visions before him, but [he practiced] in a form that had let go of all effort.

Next, I will discuss how he gradually took his three vows. In front of the sacred site of Bon ri, when he was making the great offering ritual in front of his holy father, he was given and accepted celibacy and lay vows. After that he protected his vows of celibacy from degenerating even a little, and made his monk vows a stable foundation for [his eventual] emancipation. After that he went to the institute at sMan ri Monastery, the monastery of the venerable second *Buddha* mNyam med [Shes rab rGyal mtshan]. At that point in time, when he entered into the monastic rule, he made a flower offering ritual, and also the tea offering [to the monks]. From His Holiness gShen bstan Tshul khrims dBang rgyal Rinpoche, the golden throne-holder, he took the novitiate vows in a proper way, but still kept his same name, Zla ba Grags pa. After he got his [spiritual] name, he thought it was a good omen that he kept the same name.

After that, gradually he came back to his original village. The Lord of the mDo Khams region, glorious venerable great Shar rdza, taught him the practice of *Theg chen lha'i me long* [*The Mirror of the Deities of the Higher Vehicle*], which is the practice of Lha ri gNyen po of the Me'u clan. He was given the *bodhisattva* vows, and at that time was also given the name, gZhan phan sNying po. [Shar rdza] gave him extensive advice, which he received and listened to. He received a continuation of his *bodhicitta* vows from the text of the *Byams ma* [*Loving Mother*] and from the text of the *rNam rgyal* [*Always Victorious*] systems. Then, in front of the glorious father, dBra sprul Grub chen Rinpoche, he received the great initiation for the text *gSas mkhar rinpoche sphyi spungs* [*The Precious Deity Temple of the Collected Bon Tantras*]. He extensively received this great initiation of the collected Bon *tantras* from the system of sGrub dbang. As a result of that he received a secret name, Nam mkha' sNying po. Prior to those *many* offering rituals and initiations, the initiation of the collection of peaceful and wrathful Bon *tantras* was his initial initiation. He caused that to be ripened and the agent of ripening to be ripened in his mind-stream. I heard this [directly] from him. (615)

After that, he carefully carried out all his vows and spiritual duties, especially the pure visions of seeing his root lama as an actual *Buddha*. Uninterruptedly he did daily sessions of generating his root *yi dam* and reciting [the heart *mantra*]. Because it is very important to protect one's spiritual duty pertaining to *tantra* initiations, from infancy I never disputed the spiritual duty of my *yi dam* and my lama, who had given me the initiations. Even though there are limitless stages of spiritual duties, if one has taken [vows in a way that is] not going beyond the nature of the three eternal gateways [body, speech, and mind], that is enough. Because of that, one is never separated from those [spiritual duties]. [Doing so], you almost certainly will have right speech and the right knowledge about the types of teachings [you were given] and the best practices [to be done].

By the power of his having accumulated a great amount [of merit and wisdom] throughout many lifetimes, and by his strong renunciation from the time of youth, at one point he became a homeless monk, having let go of his family. He engaged with the glory of the immortals and their eternal happiness. From childhood, he had always been taken in by many holy masters. Through his being uninterruptedly taught reading, writing, the astrological sciences, and *mandala* practices etc., the intelligence of his mind blossomed. He was protected by his vows for individual emancipation. His *bodhicitta* vows, his *tantric* vows, (616) and his spiritual duties adorned him like a rosary of jewels. Considering the way he was adorned with these [vows] and was new at them, he [clearly] showed off the best, like a three-fold awareness-holder.

1.4 The Maturation of His Spiritual Life

[Next, I will discuss] how he received the nectar of ripening [his] liberation. Initially, the way he entered into the gateway of the path of the epitome of the vehicles was in front of the keeper of the *Buddha* fields, the lord Shar rdza. There are many venerable lamas, but out of all of them, the one with the greatest kindness was this lord of the teachings during degenerate times. This refers to the second *Buddha*, the great Shar rdza Rinpoche. [This ripening] came from Shar rdza Rinpoche at a sacred site called Sha rDza at an isolated place called the Great Bliss Hermitage. [The ripening of his mind-stream occurred] when [Zla ba Grags pa] was in his meditation practice, because [Shar rdza Rinpoche] had been his karmic lama over many lifetimes. Shar rdza Rinpoche was very special to Zla ba Grags pa. It was not the same as the others, and great trust was born in his heart [even when he first met him].

When he [Zla ba Grags pa] was 17 years old, in the year of the earth-dog, he went to see his glorious lama and met him face-to-face. After that time, he relied upon Shar rdza Rinpoche as his root lama because through him Zla ba Grags pa was able to enter the gateway of the path of the unsurpassed [Great Completion] vehicle. In the *tantras* it says, "In general, the path has four possibilities: no path, wrong path, counterfeit path, and genuine path. The genuine path also has three paths: the path of renunciation, the path of transformation, and the path of liberation. Here is the great path of liberation." As this saying describes, in the *Buddha's* teachings, generally there is a distinction between external, internal, and secret categories, and between the renunciation, transformation, and liberation paths. (616) There are many ways. Among these, the epitome of all the teachings is the path of unsurpassed liberation, the teaching of Bon Great Completion. The teachings on this are very extensive, but the ones that spread throughout both Zhang Zhung and Tibet are the essence of all these teachings. From the beginning they have been taught reliably from their ancient source through an uninterrupted lineage. The ways to practice it, and the gift-waves of influence, have never degenerated. The unmistaken path travelled by all the previous ancient *Mahāsiddhas* pertains to the three—*A Khrid*, oral transmission, and Great Completion. These profound instructions are well-known.

The way of *entering* this gateway is through initiation, which affects the ripening [of the mind-stream]. Therefore, if we were to describe these [initiations] a little, [they would include] the root text on the mind-series of the great primordial *Buddha*, called the *Byang sems gab pa dgu bskor* [*The Nine Cycles of the Hidden Bodhicitta*], and the section of it called the *Sems smad sde dgu* [*The Nine Lower Mind Series*], and so forth. The great *A Khrid*, representing the enlightened intention of the Bru family, and originating from a gShen treasure, is well-known. The supreme initiation is found in the text, *gSas mkhar rinpoche sphyi spungs* [*Collection of Tantras of the Precious Temple*]. The great root initiation is from the text, *Zhi khro* [*Peaceful & Wrathful Deities*]. By receiving the great extensive adornments for great monastic practice, his ordinary three gateways [body, speech, and mind] became the definitive knowledge of having accomplished the three eternal gateways of the sacred deities. He had attained in his mind-stream extraordinary primordial wisdom derived from having gotten these initiations. In the definitive and secret unsurpassed vehicle (618) there is a teaching called the *bsGrags pa skor gsum* [*The Three Cycles of Proclamation*]. This teaching is taught in the three realms—god, *Naga*, and human. It is well-known. A text, *Yang rtse klong chen* [*The Epitome of Great Space*], has pith instructions that have been condensed from the great master Li Shus. It [originally] came from all [discovered] treasure by the *Mahāsiddha*, dNgos grub.

[The venerable lama] listened well and systematically to what was given in kindness to him, namely to the supreme initiation of his successor as in the text, *dBang khrid chen mo* [*The Great Practical Guide to the Initiations*], about the agent of ripening. Out of these texts, a text called *Zhang zhung gi bon skor* [*Four Cycles of Zhang Zhung Bon*] is especially important because it has never been hidden and is the epitome of the vehicles. This text, the *Zhang zhung snyan rgyud* [*The Oral Transmission of Zhang Zhung*], is as well-known as the sun and moon. The teachings of this tradition fall into two categories, the authoritative lineage and the experiential lineage. From the original founder of this lineage, this tradition has spread extensively and uninterruptedly up until now. The supreme initiations come from a text called *sNyan brgyud ye dbang chen mo* [*The Great Primordial Initiation of the Oral Transmission Lineage*], and the practice cycle comes from a text called the *Zhang zhung me ri* [*Fire Mountaion of Zhang Zhung*] used in order to become inseparable from the lama and *yi dam*.

By listening to the [teachings on] the four initiations and their divisions, and to the many lectures, never superfluous, used to understand their meaning, [at some point] the realization of the meaning of these initiations arose in his mind-stream. Later on, when he listened to those instructions, and also listened to lots of pointing out teachings, he was able to generate the essence of their enlightened intention. [Other than] what he had previously gotten there was nothing further to get. It was clear that the reason for saying this is because it is well-known that he had generated in his mind-stream self-occurring realization. (619)

1.5 His Practice of the Preliminary, Actual Foundational, and Concluding Practices

How he listened to the preliminary, actual foundational, and concluding practical teachings: Initially, he took as a foundation the precious pith instructions on the practical guide of *A Khrid*. His practice was in accordance with mixing both the main text and supplementary teachings of *A Khrid*. Starting with the biography of the *A Khrid* lineage masters, he got the precious pith instructions, and also [instructions on] the way to rely on the lama as a spiritual friend. Also, in the *bKa' lung rgya mtsho* [*The Ocean of Authoritative Sayings*], he listened thoroughly to the practical guide on the preliminary practices, and the stages of external and internal preliminary meditations, especially to the practical guide of the three sacred [teachings which are] staying-calming meditation, relative truth, and absolute truth. Endowed with the sacred practical instructions on *bodhicitta*, he practiced for one year and developed this practical guidance [in his meditative experience]. After that, through the unification of meditation and recitation, he practiced the way of accumulating [100,000 preliminaries] with full prostrations and an extensive *mandala* offering, and he counted only [these more difficult preliminaries] as part of his extensive [preliminary] practice.

After that, he used the main and supplemental teachings of *A Khrid*. He concentrated the mind with staying-calming meditation. Having initially done that, he extracted the benefit of concentrative-evenness, and so forth. Endowed with the supplementary cycle of the actual foundational practices he developed this practical guidance, and by that, extraordinary meditation experiences and realizations were born in his heart. Furthermore, each individual's disposition and capacity are quite different. (620) Therefore, his realization was like that of a by-passing [practitioner], and also his meditation experiences were gradually developing. That this actually happened, I heard directly from him.

After that, gradually he developed this practical guidance channel/

wind practice in a hundred-day retreat using the *Zab gter tshe dbang bod yul ma* [*The Profound Treasure of Long Life Coming from Tibet*], a text by g.Yung drung gLing pa. From the scrolls he listened to all the supplemental completion-stage practical guidance instructions, and with respect to that he did the practical guide. After that, he received the profound practical guidance of the preliminary, actual foundational, and a third from the *Rigs drug rang shyongs* [*Self-Purification of the Six Realms*] and so forth, with its ancillary teachings. He did extensive practice using these. After that, [he practiced] from the texts, *snen brgyud* [Oral Transmission], including both the complete authoritative and experiential transmissions, especially from the oral transmission lineage, and the practical guide of Bru rGyal ba. He developed this practical guidance to full measure—the preliminary, the actual foundational, and the concluding practices. He received and listened so as to have the dark retreat practical guidance from the text, *bKa' rgya ma* [*A Hundred Authoritative Words*], and then practiced it to completion.

Hereafter, the great Shar rdza Rinpoche went to a place called Nyag yul, and when returning to his own village, again, he learned the *sKu gsum rang shar* [*Self-Arising Three-fold Embodiment of Enlightenment*] that represents the enlightened intention of all the *A Khrid* and Great Completion [teachings]. He listened extensively and practiced with this practical guide. He learned Shar rdza Rinpoche's commentary, whose enlightened intention came from the expanse. (621) [This commentary] explains the three series of Great Completion. He also listened and had explained to him the *dByings rigs rin po che mdzod* [*The Precious Treasury of the Expanse and Awakened Awareness*] and did this practice for one year. He was given, listened to, and practiced from the instruction guide of the *Kun to bzang po'i snying thig* [*Heart Drops of Kun tu bZang po*]. He mixed studying with practicing, and brought it [the meaning] into his heart. Since then, he took hold of the instructions and cut off all the conceptual elaboration about these instructions. These instructions are well-known, even now.

After that, he relied only on the instructions of the precious lama Shar rdza Rinpoche, as if one [source of instruction] were enough. Then, whatever his lama said, he took it all as valid. He received the practice and manifested it in his immediate conduct, in his final goals, and continuously. He got the general teachings of the main practical guides to the three—*A Khrid*, Great Completion, and the oral transmission. The *sKu gsum rang shar* and the *Kun tu bzang po'i snying thig* are the heart-essence of these three [teachings]. He practiced these instructions as one heart teaching. Even from the words of the venerable precious lama, from amidst the assembly of limitless students, he saw him [Zla ba Grags pa] as having the best education and best meditation experiences and the best realizations. Of all these students, Shar rdza cherished him most, so he honored him and accepted him as his heart student. Even at some later point in time, when his meditation experiences and realization burst forth in the domain of space, and even when he reached the power of profound yogi conduct, (622) Zla ba Grags pa said, "This is my spiritual duty to the authoritative orders of my venerable lama, Shar rdza Rinpoche." Because of that, he never engaged in the direct [crazy] conduct of a *tantric* yogi. It seems that he said only what was sufficient as main advice, and even everything he said to others is connected with the teachings represented by the main monastery. According to the enlightened intention of his venerable lama, and according to the right time and according to his capacity, he seemed to practice the intention of the doctrine and serving the welfare of sentient beings. These are some of the points of this amazing biography.

1.6 Various Initiations and Transmissions

Next, [I will discuss] his connection to [the teachings] and how he listened to various initiations and transmissions. In front of his precious holy father, he received the peaceful and wrathful deity dBal gsas from the collection of *tantras*; and the deity dBla chen Ge khod, the deity mGar ston Phro nag, and the red and black colored deity sTag lha sPu gri. He listened to and practiced the initiations and transmissions of those. In front of the fifth Kun grol, the treasure discoverer bDud 'dul gLing pa, he received that version of the *Kun grol khrid* from the text *dmar mo 'dzub tsugs* [*Finger-Pointing at the Heart*] and the text *dMar khrid dgong pa yongs 'dus* [*Condensing the Enlightened Intention of the Heart Practical Guide*]. He listened to all the great three teachings of Great Seal [*Mahamudra*], Great Completion, and the Middle Path. From the yogi Tshul khrims dBang byug, who directly saw the *mandala* of the deity ma gyud gSang mchog mThar thug, he received the great initiation of this deity, and he received and listened to the complete practical guide and transmission of the preliminary, actual foundational, and concluding practices of the mother *tantra* system. From the effortless yogi Lhun grub Thogs med, who subdued the four demons in the expanse, (623) he received the agent of ripening through the *ḍākinī* text *mKha' 'gro'i gsang gcod* [*Secret Cutting Ritual of the Ḍākinīs*], and the cycle of *samādhi* for cutting, and the complete practice of taking malevolent places into the path; and from the emanation of Tshe dbang [Rig 'dzin] whose name is Nyi ma 'od zer, he received and listened to the channel/wind practice for ripening liberation in the text *rTsa rlung mkha' 'gro gsang mdzod* [*Secret Treasury of the Ḍākinī Channel/Wind Practice*]. From the realization-holder g.Yung drung bsTan pa he received an oral reading of all the teachings of Kun grol. From the master of accomplishments Khro sprul g.Yung drung mThong grol he received all the initiations and transmissions of the teachings of the sprul skus Blo ldan sNying po, Mi shigs, and Sangs gling; and from the great fierce treasure holder, the awareness-holder gSang sgags gLing pa, he received most of the supporting teachings for ripening liberation, namely the *A Khrid* teachings and his own rediscovered treasure teachings. From the holy great being, the sage of the sNyi wa family, Tshul khrims rNam dag, a direct student of the dBra sprul Chen bo, he received the three trainings. He received almost all of the lineage transmission of the *sutra* series, the collection series, the *tantra* series, and the mind series from the canon and the collected commentaries. Actually, here I mention these but I am worried that I am writing too much about this. Therefore, if you wish to get the details, you should look into the text called the *gSan yig* [*The Letters Heard*], which has all the details. Even though he didn't study the dialectical teachings, (624) he received numerous instructions from these teaching lineages—from the cycle of the stages of the *sutra* and *tantra* paths, especially the great texts which include all the stages of the path of the *sutra*, *tantra*, and unsurpassed Great Completion—as found, for example in [Shar rdza Rinpoche's] *sDe snod rin po che'i mdzod* [*Treasury of the Precious Three Baskets*]. He received this system of teaching to guide him. He memorized and learned it. He received [teachings on] other texts: the *Byangs sems brgya* [*Hundred Bodhicittas*] and the *lNga bcu* [*Fifty Bodhicittas*] and the *sKyabs 'gro nyi shu* [*Twenty Refuges*], and he studied and practiced them. He not only listened to them, but meditated on them gradually and with determination. After that, whatever he said, he had the wisdom to be able to explain all the *sutras* and *tantras*. Even if he gave only part of a teaching, it would convey the understanding of the main part and yielded [the result]. It appears that he was able to give that. This is the unmistaken sign of fruition of having integrated this genuine practice into his mind-stream through the gateway of reflection.

Also, even later, he acted in a manner conveying the importance of the teachings. When he met with a rare lineage of transmission or initiation, he immediately endeavored to get it. He never took it to be unimportant, and never procrastinated. If we look at the practice of present-day lamas, these lamas say how extraordinary he was. Later, after he reached forty years old, even if he didn't look at a text, his students said he had more good-hearted wisdom. (625) That means that he had internally mastered the realizations. This is a clear sign of the path toward awakening sublime knowledge, and of having it occur from his meditation experiences and realizations.

Of the unsurpassed Great Completion of all the nine vehicles, Shar rdza brings day-light to the Bon doctrines. He [Zla ba Grags pa] relied on the feet of him [Shar rdza], entered the gateway of the secret definitive doctrine, and brought about the ripening of his mind-stream through initiation. He connected to the instructions of these supreme profound paths, namely the three—*A Khrid*, Great Completion, and the oral transmission—and practiced the two stages [generation- and completion-stages]. The quintessence of the nectar of the extraordinary oral transmission filled the great vase of his heart-mind. Relying on the feet of many sacred supreme beings, and mostly relying on the four series of the great treasury of Bon, he integrated this [realization] into his mind-stream through an oral transmission and [eventually] it ripened into liberation. Doesn't he become the treasurer of millions of texts?

2.0 Meditation Practice in Retreat

[Next, I will discuss] how he practiced in retreat. Here is how he did the cycle of practices on the stages of the *sutra* and *tantra* paths: He requested individually the profound teaching of the three series of Great Completion and so forth, and connected to the way of doing the practice and using these practical instructions. He practiced in the same way as previous Bon practitioners of this lineage. You know already the kinds of recitations and practices that were described a little bit earlier, and also about his efforts using those.

Next, while he was at the mountain hermitage of Gyer sa, he completed all of the profound (626) teachings. Being exclusively in a sealed retreat, he practiced for a long period on mind-training, again as the foundation of the teaching, [relying on] the *sutra* and *tantra* stages. Initially having relied on the pith instructions that have eight, not six, he accomplished staying-calming *samādhi*-meditation. Connected with that, he did the practice carefully of the general, gradual path [designed for] three [capacities of] students; loving kindness and *bodhicitta*; and the two types of identitylessness. With respect to the way to practice, having relied upon his lama as his spiritual friend, when he did the *samādhi* of analytical meditation, he did the analysis to cultivate the characteristics of his lama and then meditated on that. After that, [he understood that] the meaning of analysis is to never be distracted anywhere else, and so he then stayed only engaged in *samādhi*-meditation. For that reason he is said to have developed definitive knowledge from the meditation experience, and that thoroughly occurred.

Similarly, since he mostly engaged in *samādhi*-meditation, he engaged mainly in non-conceptual stillness. However, it is clear that this [focus on non-conceptual stillness] is not the system of Shar rdza or the tradition of the glorious lamas of sMan Ri [Monastery].

Also, as for his accumulation-practice, most practitioners these days complete a cycle of 100,000 [practices] to purify obscurations. However, [some practitioners] view the [assignment of] 100,000 [preliminaries] as if getting sentenced by a king. [Such practitioners might be inclined to] give up practice for long periods. It shouldn't be done like this. The accumulations as part of the preliminary practices are (627) found in [all] three respective [Great Completion] systems—*A Khrid*, Great Completion, and the oral transmission—and in the mother *tantras*, and in the *dMar mo 'dzib tshugs* [*Finger-Pointing to the Heart*]. He repeated them many times, and if only the number of prostrations were added together it was said that he would have done ten million full prostrations. Also, even in his daily [practice] he did one continuous full set of preliminary practices. In the morning he offered the *mandala*, at mid-day he made offerings, in the late afternoon he accumulated [recitations of] the 100-syllable *mantra*, and in the evening he did *yi dam* practice. He continuously maintained the guru yoga as one session, and he did six sessions a day of *bodhicitta* and taking refuge. He did this according to the tradition of his venerable lama.

By doing such practices daily, [there is a risk] for greedy practitioners that the pride of having the realization will disrupt the accumulation. Zla ba Grags pa didn't do it like this at all. It is very clear that a direct realization of definitive knowledge was born from the depths about the unmistaken [relationship between the] causes and effects [of karma]. After that, having done all sorts of practices for the accumulation, and relying on the outer *tantra* ceremonies, he made a thousand offerings relying on the ritual of the eight-session prayer and the minor outer *tantra* rituals. He did them forty-nine times and, associated with that, he did the offering of the ten thousand butter lamps. The outer *tantra* ritual is derived from *Dri med gzi brjid* [*Stainless Glory—the Long Life Story sTon pa gShen rab*]. Then he gave the five endowments and the five sense-offerings, offering them ten times extensively. He did a million of each of three heart *mantras* with each individual ritual. (628) He practiced seven retreats from the *Rigs drug rang sbyongs* [*Self-Purification of the Six Realms*], and practiced the extensive fire offering from the *Kun rig las bzhi rgyun lnga* [*All-Awakened Five Enlightened Activities*], and many times the great thousand offerings from the *rNam rgyal ba'i stong mchod* [*The Thousand Offerings of the All-Victorious*]. He offered dough offerings—self-requested or requested by others—one hundred thousand times; one hundred offerings of accumulations from the mother *tantras*, done ten times; and one hundred thousand offerings of accumulations relying on the *sKu gsum rang shar* and the *bDe 'dus*. Thus, he had very many accumulations. Here, I can mention only so much.

PART III – Blue Lotus Flower: The Sacred Biography of Dawa Dragpa

3.0 **The Practice of the Approach and Accomplishment Stages**

Next, [I will discuss] how he did the practice of the approach and accomplishment stages of his particular *yi dam* deity: In an earlier and later time, while staying in an isolated place initially, the approach [practice] was condensed from the *Yab sras dril sgrub* [*The Accomplishment of Father and Son Rolled into One*], a treasure text attributed to Bon zhig g.Yung drung gLing pa, using thirty million heart *mantras*. He stayed in retreat for one hundred days using this practice ritual, and also using the *Tshe dbang yul ma* [*Long Life Ritual*]. Before this retreat, while he stayed at the abbot's residence at sTeng chen monastery, he stayed in retreat on the A bSre deities. Inside the protector temple was the peaceful deity Zhi ba brGyal ba 'dus and the wrathful deity Kho dpal gSas rngam pa. He practiced the system of their extensive heart *mantras*. After that, in addition to those, we might mention here the other deities, ritual practices, and recitations of the heart *mantra*, which would include the deity dBal chen Ge hod, the deity Me ri bKa' ma'i lugs, the deity mGar phur Zhi drag, two of the black and red swords of the sTag lha deities, and the red and black *garuda*. Using these deities, he practiced with them extensively once in every retreat. (629) I found this [fact] in his notes on his daily prayers.

Whenever he does a solitary retreat, once he seals the retreat, he follows the tradition and stays in the retreat [for the designated number of days]. He doesn't suddenly come out of the retreat. When officials and high lamas come to see him, mostly they leave without seeing him [because he doesn't break his retreat]. He relied on [Shar rdza's] *Lha gnyen shel sgong* [*Crystal Egg of the Gods and gNyan Spirits*] as the practical guide for generation- and completion-stage practice, a manual for recitation from the general collection of *tantras*, and the *Yig chung* [*Small Letters*] for the essential point of the retreat, and the oral advice on the pith instructions. Then, he did the recitation and practice using these as the main texts, especially practicing *samādhi* from the *Drug bral brgyad ldan* [*Without Six, Having Eight*]; also the unmistaken pith instructions; and associated with these, the [technique for] focusing on the object with the divine eyes of the deities with three [qualities]—clear, pure, and stable. By doing the practice like this on the three essential points, he had the experience of letting rock meet bone. Then, his clarity and stability directly reached full measure. How the signs of his individual practice occurred will be mentioned later.

Furthermore, nowadays, some who do this practice think it is a tradition just to recite *mantras* and do prayers, and think that just the musical melodies are most important. They are taken with pride. On the contrary, it is not only these [seemingly] good things, but [holding] the profound view of non-elaboration in the *dharmadhātu*, the essential point of understanding pure vision, and knowing these appearances as the deities [of the *mandala*]; (630) the profound generation-stage of the highest [*tantric*] practitioner of the inseparable pair of emptiness and appearance as the deity; and the practice which brings to the path the gift-waves of influence, such that the deities and lamas are inseparable, and so forth.

He practiced in a manner that utilized hands-on instructions on approach and accomplishment with many special teachings. For that reason, if you want to do approach and accomplishment in a proper way, I heard from the mouth of people close to him, you should be like him to practice the authentic way of this retreat. Therefore, it occurs to me that, these days, approach and accomplishment should not just be hoping [for an outcome] from just [mouthing the] words. This is the essential point to know and understand.

After that, he did the full measure of approach extensively, using the *Ma rgyud* [*Mother Tantra*], and the approach using the *mKha' 'gro gsang gcod* [*Secret Cutting Ritual of the Dākinīs*]. Sometimes, in between those approach and accomplishment [sessions], he did the practice of the red and black mule versions of the [Srid pa'i rGyal Mo] practice using the protectors of the *Buddha* doctrines, and Srid rGyal riding on a brown bear. It is clear that he did the approach and accomplishment practices on the deities and [Srid Pa'i rGyal Mo], and also on the protector Ma btsan. Later he went to lower Hor, to gTo lung, where he practiced the new treasure of dPal gter's [*Dagger Accomplishment Practice for the Threefold Embodiment of Enlightenment*], and Kun 'grol's *Ma mo rbod gtong* [*Ritual Invoking the Flesh-Eating Spirits*], and the *gDug dkar* [*White Parasol*]. Using these he practiced extensively so that the approach would reach full measure. Furthermore, it is not mentioned here, but he did many more approach and accomplishment practices that were never written down, so I didn't have the confidence to write more about them. (631)

In particular, he continued his practice in many isolated places. Since he turned seventeen years of age, up until twenty-two years of age, he stayed at the isolated hermitage of Shar rdza [Rinpoche] where he got teachings and practiced. At around thirty years of age, in particular the wood-tiger year, in accordance with previous holy lamas, he engaged in the conduct of renunciation of all worldly activities. After that he had little desire. His manner was content, open-minded, and not preoccupied. He got the enlightened intention of that. When attendants purposely tried to show what they did for him, he let them go, no longer depending on them. He remained relying on only one attendant around him to serve him while in the accomplishment retreat.

In the region of rDa khog, all kinds of lamas and reincarnated holy beings rode on horses and mules with their golden hats, etc. They had modified their dress to be "showy." It seems to me [that this showiness] was in the tradition of this region. However, our venerable lama never had the inclination or means to become vain. Furthermore, if in our mind we don't let it go of all the activities of this [ordinary] life, there is no means by which any genuine result can happen in the future. Therefore, desire is the root of *saṁsāra*. Sensory pleasures are the leaves of its poison. By knowing that, keep far away and reject: high rank (632); enjoyment of material things; servants that generate the three poisons; relatives to be taken care of; enemies to conquer; the accumulation of future plans for this life; and all [other] preoccupied activities.

It was his intention to affect the essence of accomplishment by staying in an isolated place [meditating] one-pointedly. He did it like this. Then, while at Shar rdza's mountain hermitage, Gyer Za, for his principal practice he relied on: the *sNyan brgyd rgyal ba'i phyag khrid* [*The Practical Guide of Bru rGyal ba on the Oral Transmission*], the *Yang rtse khrid gzhung* [*The Main Practical Guide of the Epitome*], and the *A khrid thun mtshams bco lnga* [*The Fifteen Sessions of A Khrid*], and the *sKu gsum rang shar gyi khrid yig* [*The Extensive Practical Guide to the Three-fold Embodiment of Enlightenment*] of the Great Completion. He needed only four sessions to develop skill.

He engaged one-pointedly, like a yogi practicing like a continuously flowing river, neither too tight nor loose all the time, without evaluating the time of the month or the time of the year.

Furthermore, most [practitioners] these days, those who call themselves realization-holders, are simply mistaken in their conduct. Their dharma-related activities have been neglected. They have become lazy, and so forth. It wasn't like this for him. As in the practice of master Shar rdza, he did some aspect of offering every day—the external and internal dough offering, the recitation to the *yi dam*, and so forth—all done diligently daily without interruption. (633) In winter, he practiced mostly separating the brightness from the dregs of [the ordinary] mind, and, for the purpose of extracting the benefit from the practice, it was very important for him to repeat many times for a month the channel/wind practice. He directly said, "There is an essential point in channel/wind practice to make a distinction between meditation experience and realization." So he made great effort on both the front and back straw practice for the downward wind channel/wind practice, and he practiced it to develop the actual signs of meditation progress, especially relying on the clear-light and illusory body. He practiced not only just general practice on this, but brought forth the clear-light by the three—entering, staying, and dissolving the wind in the central channel. From the brightness of the winds, and the liveliness of the five light-rays, he activated genuine experience on the way of arising of unification of the illusory body.

Of these [practices] even more profound was the definitive aim, the enlightened intention of the unsurpassed vehicle, the meaning of which was shown in the *dByings rig rinpoche'i mdzod* [*The Precious Treasury of the Expanse and Awakened Awareness*]. He also relied on *Kun tu bzang po'i snying thig* [*The Heart Drops of Kun tu Bzang Po*] as the extensive practical guide. By relying on these, he understood the general essential point of view, meditation, conduct, and fruition. From the perspective of the five great manners of liberation, his principal practice was to endeavor with great effort to practice thoroughly cutting through [Great Completion] with single-minded pursuit of awakened awareness. (634) At that time, in sessions both in the morning and evening, from the perspective of the three—the enlightened intention, the meaning, and acceptance—he practiced again and again to develop the skill of the four lamps practice using this profound practical guide pertaining to the four [levels of] by-passing visions. In order to extract the [full] benefit, he did it many times in dark retreat yoga. With respect to that, he continuously engaged the practice until he was thirty-eight years old.

Throughout all these many practice times, he relied upon the lama because all the positive qualities of the path of emancipation were generated from him. Therefore, he always remembered the kindness of his lama, and other than the play of the lama's enlightened body, speech, and mind, there were no other teachings and deities that existed for him. Throughout all the practices he did, he always connected to it with guru yoga using his [root] lama. Those close to him said that he did that [guru yoga] as his principal practice. This is the unmistaken essence of previous practice masters of the practice lineage.

Mostly, nowadays, there are many who make effort just part of the year to remain in practice. However, before completing the practice, some individuals develop spiritual pride about serving the welfare of others because their minds become influenced by this [pride]. [They get preoccupied with] giving the initiations and gift-waves of influence. They get far away [from the essence of practice]. One day the demons [like this] may change your mind, and then you will become desirous of all the material objects of the ordinary world. (635) Practitioners end up deceiving themselves and fooling others about the way they have done their practice. Ultimately it is rare not to be taken by demons, as rare as a daytime star. [However], this kind of venerable lama [Zla ba Grags pa] had thorough familiarity and diligent practice on this path from his previous lives. Therefore, in this life there would be no need to mention how he could ever follow after other [seemingly] wise sages who pretended or follow after other ordinary people. He said again and again that [the pride of getting caught up in serving others] becomes a hindrance to one's practice. There is little benefit even if you teach others until you have attained noble status. Therefore, he engaged mostly in sealing off his ears [and didn't teach].

Internally, he mastered his visions and overcame external appearance in what is the *dharmadhātu*. For that reason, when he did any activities of body, speech, and mind it was impossible for others to view these as misguided. He is the one who was endowed with the three—omniscience, kindness, and ability—and he generated automatically admiration and respect in all those superior or inferior. Therefore, the officials of the sDe dge region, and also the district level officials, paid their respect to this venerable lama and took orders from him. This venerable lama directly rejected the appearances of the ordinary world, and never tried to negotiate. (636) One time, authorities from sDe dge insisted that he come [and pay a visit]. He said, "I know where I should stay. If you know where I should sit, then you have to take responsibility for another's life. This wealth is like a demon beckoning you to come. You need to be careful that demons do not cause hindrances."

He never was in any way attached to belongings. Even if he got new belongings, or made refuge objects or made an offering to make a dedication to his lama, etc., there is no need to mention that the belongings he used for dedication or making refuge objects, or even the dedication letter, were such that he burned them and made a replica of the *stupa*.

Nowadays, most of the people in isolated places who take the role of a yogi, through previous bad habitual karmic tendencies and their influence, get lost in everyday busyness. Also, some don't want this, but the disposition of their minds is immature, they can't say no to others, and because of this condition, many get lost under the influence of others. This venerable master initially made a promise, and since he made the promise, if any kind of condition arose, he never went beyond his true nature. Until he attained the signs of never going back again from the confidence of his practice, he never let himself fall under the influence of distraction or cast away [his gains]. (637) Therefore, Zla ba Grags pa is like a yogi who never comes under others' influence. He is the one who seems to remain continuously in this state like the yogi 'Jig med Seng ge [the Fearless Lion].

Nowadays, most of those who enter into the path in their own mindstreams have become completely distracted by busyness and [everyday] activities. However, if they have developed the full measure of their realization, cutting through most conceptual thought and meeting with the generation- and completion-stage *samādhi* with the intention and view, they will have subdued distraction. Even for those [who have subdued distraction] there are [still] ways to go to the wrong path under unfavorable conditions. Without having such confidence, it is very difficult to get the benefit simply by intellectually understanding the teachings. Therefore, this venerable lama was a yogi of self-occurrence. He never became lazy and his practice remained focused on the accomplishment. For others, there is no need to say this, and, for that reason, the future generations also should not follow after people of pretense in these degenerate times. As told in this biography, and also in those of the previous holy masters, you need to establish your practice as described here.

Similarly, he spent all of his time only on practice. In the latter part of his life, when he was forty years old, in the year of the iron-bird, he went to the lower Hor region to gTo lung. While he stayed in one of those two isolated mountain hermitages, all the time there, whatever temporary states arose related to what he needed, he practiced short approach and accomplishment practices. He also practiced the intention toward the Bon teachings and the welfare of others. (638) In addition to that, he spent only four sessions on practice [to master it]. Therefore, nowadays, none of those retreatants can compare with his striving for accomplishment, or with the fortitude of his practice.

At around forty-eight years of age, in the year of the earth-snake, by the strength of his realization bursting forth, Zla ba Grags pa, directly realized the enlightened intention of going beyond all effort. After that, even if he did not make effort in the yoga having elaboration, he relied on that yoga like a continuously flowing river, practicing on ultimate truth. Then, only in this isolated place was he able to affect the final accomplishment of having all of his life and accomplishments being the same practice. Like this, earlier and later, at all times, he continued with great practice. There were extensive and limitless ways that meditative experiences and realization were born in his mind-stream. This venerable lama mainly holds his secret yogic conduct by meditation in his mind-stream. He stays in a way wherein he does not talk extensively to anyone.

However, like the metaphor says, "through the form of his body ['s actions] understand his mind." Similarly, how everyone came to see him and became certain about him will be described later.

4.0 Spontaneous Songs of Realization

At the time he stayed in an isolated place like that, he composed some songs of realization (639) which I have written down here. Here is the song of realization on the prayer to the lama.

> *Na Mo* Guru Rinpoche. This is the profound path of the unsurpassed vehicle. This is the precious wish-granting jewel of the three series [*A Khrid*, Great Completion, and oral transmission]. It was given to me directly from your own hands. Take care of me, kind Shar rdza.
>
> This is the best path of the secret mind of the generation- and completion-stage [*tantras*], the continuously flowing nectar of ripening and liberation. Bestow it without any effort. Take care of me, kind Shar rdza.
>
> The tracks of the path of the *Buddhas* of the three times [have been left on] the highway of genuine realization, which shows directly the unmistaken path. Take care of me, kind Shar rdza.
>
> You are the holder of the doctrines of magical Bon, the guide for the sentient beings in degenerate times, the leader of the path of emancipation for those fortunate ones. Take care of me, kind Shar rdza.
>
> I am endowed with [a precious human] body, life, and enjoyments. In every offering I am carefree and at ease. There is no way to pay you back with gratitude. I pray from the depths of my heart. Right now, in the future, and at the time of the after-death *bardos*, there is no one else other than you as the source of my hope. Therefore, look to me with unceasing compassion. May you grant me right now your gift-waves of influence.

This was sung automatically by the son of the dBra family [Zla ba

Grags ba], during practice in his retreat. (640) Again, [he composed another] like this:

> Na Mo Ci Par Ratna Ye. In the vast open space of the unborn heart-mind, comes the appearance of the light-rays of great unceasing love, and through that the sun *mandala* clears the darkness of not recognizing awakening. Take care of me, my peerless kind root lama.
>
> In front of the senses of the external clearly appearing ordinary world, appearing as a solid human appropriate to subdue, in front of me he is equal to the enlightened intention of a *Buddha*. Take care of me, my peerless kind root lama.
>
> You are the holder of the doctrines of all vehicles. The treasury of the ripening and liberation in the *sutras, tantras*, and unsurpassed [vehicles]; the teacher who guides at the right time by generating compassion; take care of me, my peerless kind root lama.
>
> The great *mandala* of the lord who holds eternity, the pillar of all the instructions of the three—*A Khrid*, Great Completion, and the oral transmission—and dispels the longing in the heart for us followers. Take care of me, my peerless kind root lama.
>
> Your enlightened intention is free from elaboration, beyond dualistic thought, and what is directly realized in itself from self-pointing out is the transparent, self-occurring, primordial wisdom of awakened awareness. May you do spontaneous consciousness-transference [manifesting] the enlightened intention of the ultimate transmission. This indestructible, primordial, secret great vehicle accomplishes the liveliness of the five self-radiant lights, and completely finishes the path of the spontaneously present four visions. May you accomplish the enlightened light body, the rainbow body. (641)

This is his prayer. The son of dBra, Nam mkha sNying po [a.k.a. Zla ba Grags pa], whatever arose in his mind he prayed like this:

> *Na Mo* Gu Ru. The natural state of primordial original purity shows its own nature nakedly. The lama's kindness can never be repaid. Take care of me Shar rdza, victorious lord. As to the elaboration of dualistic attachment to real existence, may it be cut off by the intense means of great compassion. May the enlightened intention of the clear-light of self-awakened awareness arise in my mind-stream.

Nam mkha sNying po wrote it down. He said that. This realization song served as advice to himself.

> Take refuge in the kindness of this precious lama. Make the request from the depth of your heart to cut off attachment to appearance in this lifetime. May you be given the gift-waves of influence to stay in this mountain retreat site. Here the precious human body is endowed with leisure. This [condition] is very hard to find and easy to lose. Now, if we do not make this life meaningful, how sad if we go to the next life. It is well-known that to what is called impermanent dying will come not at any certain time. Every year gets us closer and closer to dying. Right now, consider there is no time [to waste], so endeavor toward virtue. The leaders and sponsors and followers have relied again and again on one thought after another, and up to now (642) have only been distracted. Right now, become determined. If we let ourselves become influenced by the eight worldly affairs, there is no time to wake up from the harm of an idle mind. By valuing again and again minor affairs, I doubt we will go to our next lives without such affairs. Right now, in this life, totally give up hope [about worldly affairs]. We should go away from the company of humans. Remain in an indeterminate place in an isolated mountain retreat. Right now, generate the promise to stay there. This is an isolated place where there are no humans,

only an empty valley. There are no distractions by the busyness of farmers and merchants. All the time, day and night, is spent on virtue. We should be really happy to go to those kinds of places. Now there is no reason to have a lot of activities. Make a determination and keep the lama as a witness. Whether it is true or not, look into it gradually until next year. If it comes to be made up, be seized with shame. Pray to the venerable lama. With diligence practice the short *a-shay* [version] of inner fire practice. Practice is meditation on bare emptiness and awakened awareness. The mind-training is doing *bodhicitta*. The cause of subduing is to conquer the enemy of self-grasping. The cause of purification is to eradicate [suffering] with the antidote of the six realms. The aspiration prayer is to pray impartially. There is no cause to do anything beyond this. Only this time will you come to recognize your own [nature]. The mind turned inward results from the lama's kindness. Giving up the meaning of this [ordinary] life is the best aspiration. (643) May this good virtue be accomplished as your aim.

This is written by Zla ba Grags pa, the son of the dBra family. He wrote it because he was distracted by the affairs of the monastery, and to remind him of his promise about going to the mountain hermitage. The next realization song is for cultivation of the practice in isolation:

Na Mo Guru Ye. The enlightened body is the place where all refuge is gathered. To the lord of spiritual teachings who is peerless in kindness, the great powerful Shar rdza, I offer the respect and faith of the three gateways [body, speech, and mind]. The activities of this life have no essence. Whatever is done is only the cause of fatigue. Now, [I will do] the great aim of the future path. It is better to practice on the main focus. Wherever you are born in the six realms, there is no happiness. Even if happiness appears, it is also the cause of suffering. Now, [I am working for] the goal of [realizing] the essence of great bliss. It is better to hold the secure fort [of view] unchanging. There is no time. I will complete [my practice] saving face [that I have done it diligently]. Great expectation is the cause of arrogance. Now [I go] to a place where there is no connection with acquaintance [with people]. It is better to be humble and free from activities. There is no reason to have lots of attendants and disciples. That is the cause of generating distraction to self and other. Now, in not being distracted by the outside, it is better to maintain self-awakened awareness. There is no purpose to babbling with words. (644) No activities are ever finished and are the cause of [only more] fatigue. Now, [I remain] in the natural state, free of effort. It is better to do nothing and sleep naked. There is no reason to meditate with effort. Too many adjustments are the cause of conceptual thought. Now, [I remain] in the domain of space nakedly, beyond thought. It is better to cultivate the enlightened intention of Kun to bzang po. Always behave carefree and unhurried. Purposely cultivate transparent awakened awareness. Whatever happens, there is nothing to regret. In this state of bliss-mind, how amazing! This is the natural self-occurring view and meditation. I give offerings to my venerable lama. I give advice to spiritual friends. I repay the kindness to beings equal to space. From this moment on, until the end [of my life], until I become a master of the realization, [I will remain] in this place of an open isolated hermitage. May my life and practice be one-and-the-same.

This was said by the son of the dBra family, Kun bzang Nam mkha'i sNying po upon his own urging of himself.

These realization songs become the beautiful ornaments of cultivating the practices of this practice-lineage in an isolated [place]. Here, I wrote this by patiently searching through many places for the [venerable lama's] remaining letters. [I hope] those who genuinely take up the practice of these teachings of the practice-lineage will come to know them. Even if only a few such practitioners still exist, [I hope] they will admire and trust this sacred biography, and it will generate appreciation in them. This is the only place where appreciation is generated. (645) This life has little gain and lots of faults. Leave behind all activities. Do the mind-training and meditation stages of the *sutras* and *tantras*. Stay as if never satisfied with the activities of accumulation. Of the many *mandalas* of the outer and inner *tantras*, do the many recitations and meditations and ritual activities of approach and accomplishment. Connect with the *samādhi* of the three yogas. Nurture the mind in the state of genuine accomplishment at those isolated places that have been praised by former [holy masters]. Do the practice of the epitome of the vehicle and the general mind series. Spend the time day and night in celebration. Aren't you happy by always engaging in it?

5.0 How He Completed the Positive Qualities of the Signs of the Path

Next, [I will discuss] how he completed the positive qualities as signs along the path. [I will focus] here on the way he generated the usual meditation experiences and realizations. First, he stayed at an isolated place called Shar rdza .g.Yung drung Lhun po with his mind trained on the stages of meditation of the common, external and internal preliminary practices. With respect to suffering, there naturally arose [within him] an intense disgust through knowing suffering. Additionally, he generated unconstructed aversion, and through that totally cut off the conduct of attachment and desire. He could never be pleased at all with, or be in harmony with, worldly activities. For that reason he never at all did flattery in front of officials and donors. (646) He generated an unconstructed mind of renunciation. He desired to be free immediately from the places of suffering *saṁsāra*. Through that he never reflected on any of the activities of this life. Furthermore, he was perceived as a person who suffered from thirst for water [thirsting] for the next life in his spiritual practice. By the strength of that [practice], from his youth, the accumulation and practice of whatever he did was done with intense diligence, like someone whose hair had caught on fire. Especially, he practiced mind-training for a long time on loving kindness and *bodhicitta*.

[The fruition] of these arose in his heart-mind according to the stages of the path, and he took on the burden of serving the welfare of others with unconstructed *bodhicitta*, so as to possess it in his heart-mind. The power of this eradicated negative thoughts of selfish speculation. Therefore, he never did any actions [distinguishing] love for nurturing relatives and hate in conquering enemies. At the foundation [of his practice] he never acted sectarian, [making a divisive distinction between] insiders and outsiders of all schools of thought, other than the main system of his own lama. At all times he was never separated from the influence of *bodhicitta* in his heart-mind. Therefore, whatever he did became for the welfare of others. This is how his actions became [exemplary of] a biography of a holy exalted one. He became well known to everyone. Even if learned ones were to examine [his conduct], it is clear that they could see [what I mean]. Therefore, this biography is used as a main teaching text on the teachings of the victorious ones. Whatever practice he did (647) was likely associated with *samādhi*. Therefore, since his time practicing and guiding staying-calming meditation, he could remain in a single session of *samādhi* for an entire cycle of day and night. This happened many times. This is the sign of his having activated habitual karmic tendencies of familiar experiences from previous lifetimes. Generally, "*samādhi*" means being mindful [in a way that] does not forget the concentration object. Therefore, if you don't have intense mindfulness, doing daily prayers becomes associated with distractions and there is no [beneficial] outcome. He usually gave such advice. When someone did practice in front of him, if they became a little distracted, he would say, "You don't have [sufficient] *samādhi*," and would reprimand them. He reached the full measure of his practice of both the examination-meditation and *samādhi*-meditation on selflessness and emptiness. Therefore, [he saw] any external and internal substantial object as merely a form of mental labeling. Inherently nothing whatsoever existed [for him]. He achieved this [realization of emptiness] without mental construction definitively in his heart-mind. At the time of his concentrative-evenness meditation, any elaboration of dualistic thinking was reversed from its very root. By the power of this, many times in the post-*samādhi*, too, he was able to generate the meditation experience of emptiness. He was able to go out from inside his residence transparently [passing through the solid wall]. Many of his students directly saw that.

One time when he went on a pilgrimage he made a hand-print in stone. It was caused by the result of having realized genuine emptiness. (648) These kinds of descriptions came from his meditation experiences. One time he was looking at an external object and said, "I had the meditation experience of each individual and of [the] smallest of atoms [making up the object]." In saying that, we know that if we were to examine his descriptions of his meditation experiences, we would discover his [level of] mastery. His great biography depicts conduct like that found in the teachings of the victorious ones.

5.1 The Meditation Experiences and Realizations of the Path

[Next, I will discuss] how the meditation experiences and realizations associated with the extraordinary path arose. While he practiced approach and accomplishment on his individual *yi dam*, he relied on generation-stage practice through which he accomplished *samādhi*, and through that he directly achieved the eight full measures of clarity and stability. He saw [his *yi dam*] as real, with seemingly real characteristics. Those staying nearby said, "One time we were offering the father and son of Dran pa [Nam mkha'] and we saw the actual form of lama father and son Dran pa Nam mkha'." While doing a retreat on approach [using the] dPal phur deities, [those nearby] said, "We saw the wrathful form [of the deities] vividly with divine eyes." I heard them say that it was real.

Having relied upon the channel/wind practices of the completion-stage *tantras*, he separated brightness from the dregs of the [ordinary] mind. His view of emptiness [became associated with] the brightness of [an awakened] mind that is the essence of primordial wisdom. [This view] was beyond mental constructions or being dependently designated, beyond the form of a mental image, and beyond the object searched for by rational cognition and after thoughts. Its essence is directly realized naturally in its own place. Therefore, in earlier times in Zhang Zhang, a student of bSad ne Ga'u told bSad ne Ga'u, "I could stay in a single session of *samādhi* for forty days. I have achieved that ability." (649) Then, the teacher said, "If you don't have the instructions for *avadhūtī* [central channel practice], even through continuing stability of mind, you won't achieve anything." It is similar to the sayings.

If you don't extract the benefit of channel/wind practice using the mind series, then you are only practicing to have the mind stay, the mind being clear and aware. This is merely staying-calming practice, and [from this practice alone] the intention of the natural state, which is so important, will not arise. For me also, using the channel/wind instructions, I was able to get naked realization. The venerable lama had repeated this many times to his students, so it seems to be very important. Through the instructions on the method of the back straw, the upwardly and downwardly moving winds, and then by sucking in incense from the lower gate, he was able to smell incense in his nose gateway. The sign coming forth is that he could drink milk with his actual penis [by sucking it directly into the penis]. You could really see this happening. By relying on the channel/winds, if he were to rely on a [woman's] body [for sexual consort practice] he would have been able to extract the [full] benefit. I am sure that if there came a time he could do this, but it would have been harmful for him as an exemplar [because he was a celibate monk] for the general spiritual practice of [the tradition of] Shar rdza. Therefore, he never [openly] engaged in that kind of conduct. However, it is also true that he may have relied upon one or two [consorts as a] support in a hidden manner, who had co-emergent primordial wisdom. The final essential point of the secret *mantra* skillful means is beyond the basis of operation of those less fortunate. This is the amazingly great secret. (650) With respect to skillful means on the path, he practiced extracting the vital essence [fasting] for some months, not for long. He trained in the after-death *bardo* practice, and through that was able to mix *bardo* and dream practice. He told me that. Especially from the perspective of practice associated with the pair (staying-calming and special insight) and the three (setting up dismantling, and cultivating) this is how he achieved ultimate primordial wisdom. In the *Thog 'bebs* [*Direct Realization*] it says, "First, meditate on the stages of the path properly. Then, there is great benefit by increasing staying-calming and special insight. Finally, mix *samādhi* and post-*samādhi* into one. Appearance doesn't move the mind. The mind-itself without delusion becomes calm. Out of stages-versus the instantaneous-[path], this is the instantaneous [path]." While teaching this, precious lama once said that he had this kind of realization. Furthermore, through the pith instructions that distinguish between [ordinary] mind and awakened awareness, awakened awareness will [usually] subside. However, through single-minded practice in its pursuit in concentrative-evenness naked awakened awareness will arise.

In the sessions, he did skillful practice of the four [by-passing] visions, starting with awakened awareness coming to full measure. The visions in the expanse became very extensive, and this was a time when single deities arose inside and outside of the five groups of energy drops. I got this [information] from some of the spiritual brothers who were being practically guided and trained by him and who told me.

Gradually he went to the Hor region, and while he stayed at the mountain hermitage of Go mDa' (651) he became free of the outer layer of thought and desire and developed mastery on the effortless view. Even though he had good realizations that were mixed with meditation experiences, this was not the final way [for him]. In the *Thog 'bebs* [*Direct Realization*] it says, "Isn't the distinction between confidence of realization and meditation experience similar to the comparison between a *garuda* and a regular bird?" According to this saying, the way of getting the full measure of the enlightened intention of [the realization] not mixed with meditation experience is best known as coming from the realization songs, which will be described later.

After some years he went beyond even the high status of having accomplished mixing appearance and mind as one taste. Those close to him said, "One time when this lama was sitting in the sun there was no shadow associated with his body." They observed this frequently. At that time, from his own region of gNas dga' and Ga 'bam, teachers from sTeng chen Monastery along with their attendants, fourteen in all, came to see him. From his bedroom, even though the door was locked, he went out [passing right through the closed door] to the pasture. They really saw this. In his later life before he died, in the year of the dog, everyone [in the area] worried that an earthquake might or might not happen. At the time of their great doubt, many elderly people went to him and requested that through his dreams he would tell whether this would happen or not. (652) He said, "For three years I haven't had any dreams [at all]." His student, the yogi Tshul khrims 'Od zer, really heard him say that. Therefore, it is clear that from the year of the monkey he didn't have any dreams. After ending dreaming, the arising of clearlight in his deep sleep came to full measure, and was familiar to him in his meditation experience. Therefore, this is the way the definitive signs came to him regarding reaching enlightenment in this very life. In the *tantras* it says, "Those of best capacity end dreaming and dissolve into the expanse." According to this saying, he had now reached the boundary. By relying on that, he had the great sign of practice reaching its endpoint of the path. This has been talked about extensively, but I won't elaborate here.

5.2 **Common Signs of Accomplishment**

Here we will talk a little bit about other common signs of accomplishment. Generally, this kind of venerable lama would have shown off the best of the positive qualities of his highest internal realizations. There are many wondrous common signs of accomplishment and there is no need to be amazed, but for some ordinary people I will describe some of these. When he was a youth and was inside the protector temple of sTen chen [monastery], when he was practicing the approach and accomplishment of the deity dPal gSas, the ritual attendant really saw lights of fire coming from his drum and bell. While in the mountain hermitage, at the time of practicing approach and accomplishment using the deity dBal Phur, at the back side of the hermitage a large boulder came rolling down, and just by his pointing his finger at it, it stopped rolling. Everyone there was so amazed!

On the day of the ritual for taking blessed food, (653) a kite and eagle were hovering in the sky and a wolf came around. These were seen as special signs. One time, on the 10th day of the lunar calendar, when he was making a ritual offering according to the text, *Yab sras dril sgrub* [*The Ritual Practice the Father and Son Bell*], the Tibetan beer filling a skull offering bowl suddenly turned the color of milk, and after that the outside and inside of the practice place everywhere was saturated with perfume. Whoever happened to be present was given a spoon of the beer and, because of that, everyone said it had a special taste no one had ever experienced in this life. When doing the ritual offering of the mother *tantra*, one time during the offering, from the south of the *mandala* a rainbow occurred, and another [smaller] rainbow started rotating around the ritual vase. Everyone saw this. There are many [incidents] like this.

Later in his life he went to Hor Brag mGor, and while there he came directly before the Chinese *Mahāsiddha* named Rdo rje Don grub. This *Mahāsiddha* was in a crazy form. Even so, he received this lama in a traditional way. Then, they went into a dark cave. The fire there was covered with ashes. Then, he [Zla ba Grags pa] sat on top of it [the fire] for a long time, and because of that red sparks directly occurred; even so, they never touched his body or clothes. There is no need to say this. Everyone was amazed. Then, the [crazy] *Mahāsiddha* prostrated to the lama [Zla ba Grags pa] and gave him the name Pema Rigs 'dzin. After that, the same *Mahāsiddha* got up and made a big fire in the stove. (654) Sometimes the venerable lama put his leg in the fire, and sometimes his hand stirred the fire, and even so his hand certainly never got burned.

One time he went begging in the Brag mGo region, and while in Shar Thang he went to the house of a Chinese reincarnate lama. Before he went there a woman came to the house and said, "Zla ba Grag pa will come. Be prepared." Later, he said this woman was one of the Bon protectors, sGra bLa Mo. Once when the army of China was stirred up, he went to gTo mDa' Monastery. A person riding on a red horse was coming to receive him. Later, when they got closer [to the person], he was an unknown person. They asked the reason that the man was here. He directly said, this is surely one of our protectors.

While he stayed in the monastery, a hunter and hunting dog were given a protection thread. Since then, the dog stopped chasing after wild animals. So the hunter offered the dog to the lama. This dog is like those people who have faith in the lama, and for those who didn't have faith in the lama, the dog bit them.

A person called mKhar rab Chos Skongs came from a lama residence called Snyi Khog Lo dGu to invite him. He brought a horse. On the way they came to a cliff called Chu bSur and when they arrived there he was no longer on the horse. When the man looked far away, the man saw him the distance of an arrow shot far away [on the other side of the cliff]. He was sitting there. The man really saw this. (655)

At that time, a monk from the monastery of Brag mGo named g.Yung Lo went to the main monastery and asked the venerable lama to give him his own hair. Then, with a knife he cut off his hair and gave it in a folded paper to the man. After four years at the main monastery, he opened the folded paper and it had become many relics [white small balls]. The hair he had given to his friends [earlier] had also become a relic. I heard them talk about this.

A little while later, at one point he was sitting in the town of rBa mDa'. A venerable lama had passed away called Tshul khrims rNam dag, so he did a ritual for the deceased. Without any fire from the butter lamp [the paper with the lama's identifying information on it] caught on fire by itself. I heard this from a person called mGar ba Ao rGyan skyab and the monk called gSang sNags.

Some time later, he was invited to a valley called rBa mDa' gNas Kho. There was a very small retreat cave. He went there. Nearby on the rock he drew a swastika and the letter *RA* with his finger. After that, he went into the cave and vanished. Others searched everywhere, inside and outside [the cave], but couldn't find him. After awhile he went right through the rocks and popped up at the summit of the mountain called Kyung gDor [*Garuda*-faced mountain]. His students, sMon lam gTsug phud and Tshul khrims Grags pa and others, all saw this directly. (656)

Again, one time in a family called Tsha mDa' Tshang, there was a lama/doctor from the Sa sKya school there whose name was Tshe dbang Phun tshogs. Zla ba Grags ba said to the doctor, "Either I will come to you or you can come to me." Then, this doctor came before him. The doctor saw him manifesting as [the Sa sKya deity] gSang bdag Phyag rdor. [The doctor] developed great faith in his heart. He told everybody about it.

Furthermore, elderly people told many stories like this about him, although I didn't write about them here, but you can believe that I will write more about this later.

There is a saying, "Yogis don't want the signs, but the signs want the yogi." Similarly, he purposely never showed paranormal abilities or the magical display, etc., but even if he didn't wish to, [these abilities] incidentally happened. Through relying on these he became a famous *Mahāsiddha*. Related to this, some of his songs of realization were born through his meditation experiences and realizations:

> *A Ho!* The guides are from the fortunate pure realm, the teachers of the three-fold embodiment of enlightenment. The definitive meaning, secret, and unsurpassed [vehicles] are the sources from which the lamas of the three lineages came. You are the successor of the oral transmission lineage for the liberation of the enlightened light body [rainbow body], absent any outflows. [657] The great Shar rdza's kindness is greater than anyone's. The eternal teachings are not constructed through reasoning. The gift-waves of these and the three series of Great Completion teachings will never disappear. The unmistaken tradition of the practice lineage is the practice of *A Khrid* and Great Completion. In this very lifetime, holding *Buddhahood* is through the *Kun tu bzang po'i snying thig* [*Heart Drops of Kun tu bzang po*]. Awakened awareness is primordial, purified from deluded appearance, and is beyond conceptual thought. Meditation settles into itself without the progression of *samādhi* and post-*samādhi*. This is self-liberating conduct that is maintained automatically and unceasingly. The fruition is the direct realization of the self-abiding natural state. This is the highest vehicle for the yogi who holds stability in *saṁsāra* in this very life. The yogi who stays in the valley free of activity activates the meditative experiences and realizations internally. This awareness-holder of the *tantras* sees the seemingly appearing world as the pure lands. This is the secret path of skillful means from which co-emergent primordial wisdom arises. It is the *tantra* that consumes the sense-pleasures as a sacred food. It is the *samādhi* of the intention and view that transforms actions into accumulation. It is the good path of *bodhicitta* that does

away with self-importance. It is the meaningful devotional prayer that accomplishes the welfare of self and other. I am the fortunate yogi who completes [enlightenment] in a single life. Appearance, which is the liveliness of awakened awareness, arises in my mind with joyful experience. (658) It is like a small melody that spontaneously sings about whatever arises in the mind. A yogi naturally sang this from his comfortable bed.

This song of realization comes from the isolated place of gTo gLing [when he was] singing about whatever came into his mind. Here is another realization song about his happy realization:

Venerable genuine *Buddha* of complete victory. He is called the great Shar rdza, a well-known name. May you look at me, your spiritual son, uninterruptedly. May you grant me the gift-waves of influence in my mind-stream. I have definitely attained a human body with its leisure and endowments without holding the inherited house of self-grasping. I endeavor again and again to be afraid of the future. Right now I have cut off being wrapped up in attachment to this life. I am certain that I left my homeland where I was born. I do not hold as my basis any other place either. Where ever I am, I happily make it over and over again as my homeland. Right now I am free from being wrapped up in attachment to sense objects. I left the monasteries where I was self-grasping. I am not sectarian about any school or view. I have meditated again and again on my belief in pure vision. Now I have no more desire or hatred in the place where I stay. I have left the belongings I had collected. Without any pretentious thought toward others I make friends over and over again with [the state of] satisfaction. (659) Now, I have become free from holding onto wealth. I have given up friends and students. Not having to be mindful of the abilities of high people, I am the servant only to myself. Now, I am completely free of attendants surrounding me. I have requested the ripening liberation of the *sutras* and *tantras*. I do not spend my life in empty talk. I practice again and again diligently. Now, the meaning of what I heard comes into my mind-stream. By making a request to the lama and *yi dam*, without making any distinction between good and bad, I meditate again and again continuously with my lama on my crown. Now, the gifts-waves of the lineage fall upon me. By diligently doing the channel/wind practice, without staying-calming meditation with its grasping-mind, I have separated out over and over again the brightness [of awakening] and the dregs in my own ordinary mind. Now, primordial wisdom arises from the depths. I endeavor to focus the mind on this aim. I have no intention to boast about ideas. Practicing over and over to mix [awakened awareness] into the state of sleep, now I have mastered the clear-light of dreaming. By virtue of doing the practice of Great Completion, in the view I never mentally construct with thought, and by differentiating again and again between the ordinary mind and awakened awareness, now I come to bare awakened awareness. I reject over and over again actions based on thought elaboration. (660) I don't get lost in a meaningless vast void. By sleeping again and again in a state free of elaboration, now I am happy when sick, when joyful, and when dying. Practicing this way, I recognize [I am always happy]. I don't expect the gain or loss of some final happiness. Right now I only seek immediate happiness [not some final state]. Other people [who search for some final state] are not inside their hearts. These days, in this seemingly existing world, there is no happiness more than one's name, and thus I am [singing from afar with a happy mind. I aspire to spend my life in this isolated place.

Kun bzang Nam mkha' sNying po sang this song when he was really happy, when he was forty-eight years old, staying at a mountain retreat in rBa mDar. Again, another song:

A Ho! This impure deluded thought and pure victorious primordial wisdom, both in the natural awakened awareness, are one. There is no need for a path of renunciation or a path of transformation. Harm by various influences and negative forces, and the signs of the path as bliss, luminosity and non-conceptual stillness, both [negative and positive] are the same liveliness of the play of bright awakened awareness. Therefore, there is no use to [the mental engagement of] accepting and rejecting. Both thought elaboration with respect to perceptual objects, and being without [extraneous] conceptual thought, sayings, reflections, and expressions, are all the same natural state of awakened awareness. (661) It is unnecessary to go to pleasant or unpleasant places. The elaboration of the four extremes—eternalism, nihilism etc.—and the middle path beyond all extremes, are both the same state of transparent awakened awareness. It is unnecessary to validate or invalidate [different] spiritual traditions. What exists, exists. What does not exist, does not exist. Therefore, what am I to do about the spiritual tradition of appearance versus emptiness? There is no existence and no non-existence. What am I to do with these words and labels, which are beyond any object of conceptual thought as the transparent, self-occurring, primordial wisdom of awakened awareness? This great land, whose place *is* the natural state, is where this yogi who remains loose is happy.

He just says whatever feels comfortable. These are the profound realization songs that burst forth from the enlightened intention of his meditation experience. Through them you encounter faith. Similarly, here he is talking a little about the stages of the signs along the path. In the *rTogs tshad gsal sgron* [*The Clear Lamp of the Full Measure of the Realization*] it says, "Genuine practice is never lost. Therefore, having the full measure of the signs is very important." According to this passage, having reflected on this reason, I noted just some of the stages of signs along the path.

[This practice pertains to] disgust with and renunciation of the places of *saṁsāra*, and taking responsibility for the welfare of others with compassion and *bodhicitta*, using the profound view free from all elaboration. (662) These aims are drawn into the heart-minds so as to increase them. This yogi has attained the sign of seeing the deities. Having mastered the mixing of both the upper and lower channels/winds, with awakened awareness bare and stripped [of conceptual thought], he exhausted all deluded dreams. There are immeasurable positive qualities along this amazing path. With the intention of mixing appearance and mind into one taste, he mastered all the external and internal elements, and through that came all sorts of marks and signs of amazing accomplishments. When people talk about the foundation of his [practice] all over the country it is pleasant to hear.

6.0 Attaining the Accomplishment

[Next, I will discuss] how he attained the accomplishment through the profound treasure of [having received] the gift-waves of influence. In general, [I will discuss] how he received the prophesies of the realization-holders and the *ḍākinī*s. When he was staying at the mountain retreat of Shar rdza, while practicing the approach and accomplishment on the deity Tshe dbang Rig 'dzin, in the manner of staring immediately into awakened awareness, his eyes gazed into space [and actually saw Tshe dbang] there. While reciting the *mantra*, "*Tshe dbang gsal 'bar...,*" etc., with palms joined together [praying], he said again and again, "I pray to the lama Tshe dbang Rig 'dzin who is the protector of sentient beings. In all times and situations I follow you. May you grant me, without remainder, the initiations and accomplishments of enlightened body, speech, and mind." Staying nearby, some of his students saw and heard this, but were unable to ask him how it happened. The fact that he saw master Tshe dbang face-to-face is a very extraordinary occurrence. (663) Later, when he went to the Hor region, while in lower Hor in a place called Dre'u mDo, he suddenly said, "We should stay here." Purposely facing in the direction of gNas gSar, he went and stayed seven days in that sacred place. It was said that he drew a swastika counter-clockwise by hand in the meditation cave. In this sacred place he had visions of the spiritual father and son of the great lama Dran pa Nam mkha'. Then, the great lama Dran pa told him that he had prophesized that this mountain was a sacred place, and that this was the sacred place of the heart deity gTso mTshog. This was seen on scrolled paper where there was a story about the special visions that had occurred. Because it was only partially auspicious, [the scroll] did not last to be helpful to sentient beings. Later, there was nothing left of the manuscript to see.

While he was sitting in an isolated place in gTo Lung, there was a scripture called the *Dakki'i zab gsang lung gi gtam* [*The Profound Sacred Prophesy of the Ḍākinīs*] that described how to recognize someone from a noble family. Having relied on that, he brought forth the skill of enlightened intention and how he should develop the immediate cause of that. There was a list of prophesies about that. I heard about it and saw it, but now I don't see it anywhere.

While he was staying in the house of a sponsor, whose name was mGon po bKra' shis, in a place called rBa mDa' he received a prophesy that people on the frontiers will come and change the times [by war]. He wrote these prophesies down by hand and put them into a wall. (664) Not very long after, the war with the Chinese broke out.

Similar to this, he saw visions of *ḍākinī*s and awareness-holders giving the gift-waves of influence, prophesizing about the future, and so forth. There are many occurrences like this, but the lama didn't look into it. Therefore, I didn't put it in the notes, and no one had asked him write it down. There is only this much [to say].

6.1 How the Profound Treasures Came Forth

[Next, I will discuss] specifically how some of the profound treasures were discovered. In general, [let me begin by discussing] the meaning of what is called "a profound treasure." He received initiations and instructions directly from earlier *Mahāsiddhas*, the three immortals, the father and two sons of [Dran pa Nam mkha'], etc., with the enlightened intention for the purpose of the future, and giving the seals to the sacred treasure keepers, and similarly making aspiration for the occurrence of serving the welfare of sentient beings. That occured through relying on those causes. Also, his realization was equivalent to that of the heroes [awareness-holders] and the *ḍākinī*s who are on that level. This is the basis of operation for those of fortunate karmic connection.

This lama, even if he didn't serve the welfare of sentient beings greatly by discovering many profound treasures, I will tell about some of what happened. One time he went to a mountain called Bla ri dMar Brag, associated with the deity Dam can. He went with his brother g.Yung drung rGyal mtshan and his student Tshul khrims 'Od zer. In the company of those two [at that site he pulled a stone box] from the rock [and nearby was a paper describing] how to open the stone box. (665) When they opened it, inside was a small *vajra* wrapped in yellow paper. Furthermore, there was a small box made of white crystal and a golden statue [covered] with new frost. He took them out from there. Later, using the yellow paper that the *vajra* was wrapped in, he wrote down a short prayer to Guru Rinpoche called *bsam pa lhun grub* [*Spontaneous Reflections*] and gave it to everyone. He put that small crystal box inside a *stupa* in rDza Khog. After the lama passed, the golden statue was never seen again. Either the owner of the treasure [the deity] took it back, or he returned it as a treasure. I don't know exactly what happened.

From the mountain behind the mountain retreat at rBa mD'a, [at the site of] the rock with the *garuda* face, he pulled out a black stone box with a white drawing of the letter *MA* written in *gshur ma* script, and the image of a sun and moon. Inside it there was a text about the rNam sras deity, but he didn't copy it.

In the Hor region there is a mountain called Dre'u mDor. At the base is a rock. When they arrived at the base of that rock, a door in the rock face opened by itself about the height of a person above [the base of] the rock face. At that time the brother of g.Yung drung rGyal mtshan lifted the venerable lama upon his shoulders, and, when his hand reached in the door, he took out a stone box. He said this box was called the "essence of black earth." Then, after closing the rock door, it was said that there was no trace [of any door left].

Furthermore, while he went to the place described above called gNas gSar, he went with a monk called g.Yung drung 'Od zer (666) and took from that rock a black stone box. Inside the box was a text about a wrathful lama Bla ma Drag Po, but he didn't copy it down. In a place called rBa mDa', above a path on the cliff, is a meditation cave of lama g.Yu sgra sNying po. There he took a stone box with the letter *BE* on it along with a drawing of a three-winged yin-yang symbol.

While in gTo Khog, at one time he said he should go to the meditation cave of lama rTsa ra 'Od zer rGyal mtshan in a valley nearby g.Yung drung gLing monastery. He took along his student called bKra' shis Don grub and went there. The lama was approaching the monastery, so they welcomed him with incense. The smoke circled around as if circumambulating this holy place. On the way there were big patches of ice [that were dangerous], but he let his horse gallop on it very fast. Then, they saw lots of rainbows spreading. From this cave he took an amazing iron dagger. Sometime later, from the ear of the deity-hat [carved on the top of the dagger] came a spontaneously appearing medicinal powder. Nearby is a place called Khro tshang sNgang where there is a spring of water. From inside that [spring] he took out a box of sealing wax. There is another Srig pa'i rGyal Mo meditation cave called Srid rgyal sGrub phug. From there he took a stone box which had the letter *DHA* written on it. The monk g.Yung drung Shes rab, etc., witnessed this, and it was brought in front of them. I heard it like that. (667)

After that, while he was staying at the mountain retreat at rBa mDa', he went to the mountain peak of Khyung gDong. His teacher who was called Tshe ring bKra' shis made an incense offering [to the deities], and through that, out of the empty space, came a sound "*ZIR*", and then the form of a box appeared in his hand. Then, at a distance of three spear-lengths, powdered stone began to fall like snow. They took it. The people who were nearby are still around, and they said they still have the powder.

One time in a place called mNga' ris, while he was teaching preliminary practices as the abbot-in-residence for nine years, there was a lama from the family lineage lama of Dre'u ston. At the front of his table, a statue of Dzam nag fell onto the table with the sound, "*THEG.*" All the students who were there saw it happen. There are many stories like this.

He composed from the treasure teachings previously mentioned in the prayer to Guru Rinpoche, *bsam lhun*... another treasure text called the *Zab gcod* [*Profound Cutting*] associated with the deity Thugs rje kun Srol, along with its supplementary text [which he also composed]. Now also, he is continuously serving the welfare of all sentient beings through these texts. Many others are still practicing ripening and liberating using these texts. I never found more [texts] than these. He had taken most of the statues and boxes to rDza Khog and placed them in a *stupa* there.

7.0 Various Visions

[Next, I will discuss] a little about his manner of having seen various visions. While staying in rJa Khog, while he was in a retreat using the text *Rigs drug rang sbyong* [*Self-Purifying the Six Realms*], on the six sites of his body he saw the six seed-syllables (668) in the form of light, and from there various visions of the six realms arose. One time, during his channel/wind practice, he wasn't able to distinguish whether these were real or just visions, but his body was adorned with a swastika, and in the three main channels and the five *chakras* limitless visions occurred in the gateways of arising. One time, when he was at gTo mDar, his students, Tshe dbang bStan 'dzin, Blo bzang Shes rab and others, were gathering together making noodle soup. Suddenly, he asked them to make a great burnt offering. Then, they dedicated the burnt offering and recited the one thousand syllable *mantra*. While doing the dedication they said that the venerable lama mentioned the name of a person who had passed away called Sod nams mGon Po. He really did that. Also, he said, "Leave the noodle soup near the door [for the dead person]." While he was making the dedication they didn't see [the deceased person's] form-body, but everyone who was there really heard many [deceased] people talking together. Then, he put his shawl over his head and he cried a lot, and he said, "What pity for the beings of the after-death states and the lower realms," and he repeated this over and over again. He had visions of the after-death states and of the lower realms. This really happened, but there is nothing written about this.

One time while in rBa mDar, while he was staying with his sponsor mGon Po bKra' shis, right after a late afternoon session (669) he did extensive cutting practice [*gcod*]. When asked the reason why, he said "Here comes a dead person named sNgo Na." That is why he did the cutting practice. The next day just around sunrise a person came to make an offering and said, "A person named sNgo Na has died." These kinds of things happened many times, but sometimes, when some asked the lama the reason why, he answered [humbly], "The winds in my channels are weak and that accounts for most of the visions seen, and there is nothing to focus on [as important]." He purposely didn't want to talk about it [and make a big deal over it]. This event wasn't written down. Therefore, I only got this much and didn't write more than this.

From the expanse, three immortal awareness-holders showed their faces because they were happy with the ritual offerings to the deities and the lama. They showed themselves directly to him and gave him the gift-waves of influence. Certain prophecies were shown and also masters of the treasures [appeared]. The gift-waves of influence were given by these previous awareness-holders. It was the [right] time for the *ḍākinīs* and protectors to open the seals [on the treasures]. He received the refuge objects, sacred substances, profound teachings, and many profound treasures and accomplishments without effort. In his internal body as the swastika, the high and low, pure and impure visions appeared, the beings of the after-death states, and so forth. Many other visions came. The manner of arising of these amazing sights is inconceivable.

8.0 Serving the Welfare of Sentient Beings

Next, [I will discuss] how he served the welfare of sentient beings and the teachings in all sorts of ways, (670) [beginning with] describing how he worked for his own monastery at one time. When the venerable lama was twenty-two years old, the reincarnation of dBra sprul Rinpoche, called sKal bzang bsTan pa'i Nyi ma, was born. When he was six years old, his own monastery, sTeng Che Monastery, had a significant problem [caused by] envy by another [competing] system that caused [the opponents] to [attack and damage the monastery]. dBra's [teacher's teacher], his highness, the holy elder, master teacher, whose name was g.Yung drung bsTan pa, ordered him to go with him to Nyag shod. They both went there to the seat of the regional government and met the official, whose name was mKhan tshung bSod nam rGyal mtshan pa. While he was talking about the affairs of the monastery, the butter lamp on the table lit by itself. The venerable lama had shown his [paranormal] signs of accomplishment so that the officials had great faith in him. They listened and were willing to do whatever he wanted. Because of that, they were able to inform the Dalai Lama [directly], so they submitted the request to the Dalai Lama and from him got the permission [to rebuild the damaged monastery]. When the monastery was being constructed again, the local people and officials of the Hor region were ordered to serve, and the [newly built] temple, the abbot residence, and monk residence were re-established, better than before. He [the Dalai Lama] helped. (671)

One time, while at the rJe Sor mountain retreat, he helped to build the statue of mNyam med gShen rab rGyal mtshan. He helped paint the mural of *yi dams* on the dome. He gave the Bon canon. He gave sixteen practice texts. Out of his kindness he gave whatever he had to make it happen.

When around forty years of age, at mid-life, according to the urging and prophesies of the deities and lamas, he went to the lower Hor region and went to a monastery called Shel khog rGya rong. While there, a girl who was not so attractive came to receive him. They went together a little way and then she disappeared. He said that she was one of the protectors, Ma Mo Drel dMar, on her red mule. At this very monastery, there was a monk from a family lineage called Tha lta Khyung 'phags Hra mo from the Khyung po region. He had four brothers. Among those four there was geshe Tsa'i nang so Dam po, or [also named] g.Yung drung Ye shes. He built the monastery. Later, it had deteriorated, and it was not operating well at the time. He had a dream about Ma Mo wherein she urged him to rebuild. First, he gathered all the people and he gave them teachings for a month about the preliminary practices, and then ordered them to do the work for the monastery. There was only one floor to the temple, so he put on a second floor. (672) Inside he made a statute of sTon pa gShen rab in a monk form called Khro gtsug rGyal ba, and painted the murals and wood until the temple was completed. Then, he did a ritual every day in the protector temple. Also he did the approach and accomplishment for the *yi dam* deities, and also made offerings every day to the protectors. He gave to them all the sacred substances they needed. He said that from that day the monks and lay people should be separated. The monastery should continue, and the monk precepts should be maintained. He taught extensively about the system of the main monastery—the rules of how to assemble, the annual rituals, especially those that young monks should study—and that the teachers should do a retreat on the approach to and accomplishment of [the deities]. Even though he made a code of ethics for the monastery and gave advice, he made it so the doctrine and teaching progressed from the foundation upwards. At that time some asked him, "If we do the practice of Bon in a genuine way, what would that way be?" He answered, "All the time your mind should tend toward virtue, and whosoever does that it is called 'Bon.'" But the dialectical monks said, if a basis exists, it should be *Bon* and *Chos*. What he taught is a little different from that. He answered, "What is called 'practicing Bon' means that if your own mind-stream tends toward virtue and mixes with it, then that is the practice of Bon." Therefore, he always talked in a genuine way.

These days, when lamas give spiritual advice and transmissions from their thrones according to the main texts, they draw forth appreciation at once. However, one day a more serious time will come (673) [when they stop doing this], and if you were to ask them privately about this, they would say, "There is no other choice." [Such an answer] would just be the advice of worldly [not spiritual] people, and is just the behavior of divisive talk. His followers who relied on him never heard those kinds of things from this venerable lama.

While he was in that monastery, whatever things he got were donated to the monastery, and, as mentioned before, whatever else [like donations] he received, he used as a money-offering or tea-offering to the monks. Associated with that, the foundation of the *Buddha*'s teachings, is the assembly of monks. He understood the enlightened intention of this, so that in many different monasteries he made donations and offered the [three] refuge objects—enlightened body, speech, and mind—and he gave money-donations and tea-offerings [to the monks]. He did many things like this. He never said anything good or bad to the lamas and monks. When he met with the assembly of monks, he bowed, made prostrations, and so forth, since in his previous life he had the disposition to be [already] familiar with the behavior of holy people. Everybody talked about this. At that time, and earlier or later, any kind of object or things he got, he never kept it for himself. Furthermore, he thought they should be used to accumulate merit for self and others. (674) Even small things should not be given to the wrong place, and should never go to waste. He exchanged them for holy objects, and gave them to others who needed them and made a ritual offering of them. Furthermore, any kind of animal he got [as a gift], he said, "Now these animals have been rescued and there is no way to sell them to others." If he got a female yak or a goat or a sheep, he had someone cut the fur and long hair and made a handle of *zo dar*[4] and, because he and the animal were [karmically] connected, he did a dedication.

Any kind of weapon he bought, even if it was expensive, he immediately dismantled, and made it into a chisel to carve stone. When he wanted to make a replica, he dug the mud by hand. He never had the disposition of someone pretentious, haughty, or acting like a child. Additionally, his view was even higher than the sky, but his conduct was careful. His biography is very clean, and commands respect. It seems to remain amazing. The way he made offerings with all these things will be shown later.

9.0 Serving the Welfare of Followers in Different Places

9.1 Serving Followers in Different Places

[Next, I will discuss] how he served the welfare of sentient beings individually, and of many followers in different places. This venerable lama said, "Whatever you do, work and other activities, if you are influenced by generating *bodhicitta*, then whatever you do becomes an offering." Whatever teachings you do for the welfare of others, if there is no dedication it only accomplishes the aims of the self, and doesn't become enlightenment." (675) He always used to say, "When we examine this, there is nothing else to do other than for the welfare of sentient beings." When he arrived he gave advice, urging others to act virtuously. Now I want to write down the ways he gave advice and served others.

---

4. Unclear what this word is.

While staying at rDza Khog from the time of his childhood, the dBra family was such that he was the son of an official, so they paid respect. Below the monastery he helped the spiritual subjects to do rituals, give initiations, and so forth, and through that he benefitted many beings. If we were to talk about the general way of the lamas, there are too many ways. It is not very important [what they did in general], so I didn't mention it here.

When a new monastery was being built, it was because the monastery purposely urged him to do this for them. He went everywhere in upper and lower rDza. He went around sTong zer, in dGe rTsa brDa Thar, also to upper and lower Yid Lhung, and so forth, to collect donations and to bring success to what he wished. When he went to a guest-house, he did whatever [ritual] the [inn keeper] wanted, like doing an incense offering to the local deities. In the village he did a ritual for prosperity. If someone had a short life span, he did a long-life ritual. For the deceased he did dedications and burnt offerings. For non-humans he did the cutting ritual. When people gathered he gave the transmissions on the meditation stages and the three heart *mantras*. He gave lay people one-day precepts and fasting practices, and he urged them to do daily prayers. He gave freedom [to animals]. He encouraged them [his students] as much as he could. He gave them sacred substances to taste that helped them become liberated. (676) He did this every day.

Furthermore, at this time his life story had never been clouded by wrong motivation while doing Bon practices, such as doing them with the five wrong livelihoods or doing the practices out of greed. Not doing these things was co-emergent [with his on-going] practice. He was the one doing this and that is why he is a source of faith [for others]. At that time, while he went to the nomad village dGe rTse, he sent one monk there with three mules with full packs. The monk was robbed and killed. He tracked down and recognized the robber. This could have been the foundation for strong anger, but he said, "It is better to remain, and be completely patient." Those kinds of events I witnessed.

Furthermore, if I were to mention one or two additional specific examples, in the rDa gTu area, a big disaster [drought] happened. All the people were very despondent. Even all the great lamas were helpless at the time. He went there and did a rain-calling ritual. He went to the top of a hill to the center. There was a woman from the dBar family called g.Yung drung Lha mo. She was a *ḍākinī*. He did extensive ritual offerings to the *Nagas*, and at the end did a rain-calling prayer. By just doing that, suddenly all the clouds gathered and heavy rain came, and [the villagers] were spared from their fear. At that time, there was a spring nearby and he stayed there for awhile. Emerging out of the spring and then rolling into his hand was a white conch. (677) Everybody saw that. Since then, this venerable lama became well-known for his spiritual power.

One time he went to Nyag Shod for the purpose of [visiting] the monastery there. A powerful officer there from the Guru dPon family called A rTa kept repeatedly asking him to do practice for him so he did the accomplishment practice associated with the black dagger deity at that time. Seemingly agitated, he was practicing from a section of a text on grabbing and deliberately [roping in], and at one moment, in a manner that [seemed] angry, he took a sword in his hand and threw it upward, and when the sword was falling back to the ground it took the form of being twisted in a knot. [They asked him why he did that and] he said that below his family house there was a forest and he saw a woman [sorceress] leaving carrying a human head. At that time the official said that in an earlier time, because of this woman, nine people got trapped in the trees and had died untimely deaths. He said, "Bring a shaving of that wood." Then, he used it as a concentration object, and did a ritual for subduing and guiding, and through that it stopped the untimely dying of others there [at that site]. He did great benefit [for the local inhabitants].

After visiting the Hor region, at a monastery called bKra' shis sMin grol gLing, he did an official monastery ritual using the text called *Khong spungs gtad sprugs* [*Stirring Up the Curse Using Dran pa Nam mkha'*] emanating from the *mandala* in front it looked like a star with a sphere of light appearing like a plate with lots of light falling upon it, and then it rose up through the dome [of the temple] and (678) disappeared in the sky. Everybody saw this directly. The venerable lama said, "In another time one or two curses were made, but at this time there are the [favorable] signs of the benefit of being free from those."

One time, at Dre Shod in upper Hor, there was a woman whose family name was Bod dgon Tshang who was suffering from mental illness. Some monks—Sku zhas gZigs rgya, 'Khrungs gsar, and others—tried to heal her but couldn't, and she remained like that. Another lama said, "If you invite the lama from the dBra family, the spiritual son Zla ba Grags, it could be useful." So, he was invited and went there. Then, he did a cutting practice, and the spirit was brought under control, and then all the ropes binding [the crazy woman] snapped, and she was released, and while running she made the sound *"AUR LING DER,"* and she came in front of him. She did this at the time he was saying the prayer, "Listen to the order," and at that very moment she came to him at that very sentence. Then, immediately her craziness was subdued, and she was sitting with her hands together [in praying position]. Then, one of the elderly people said, "Oh, this lama is very powerful. When he told her to sit down, she did." Since then, her mental illness was cured in its very foundation, and because of that some people called him the "lama subduer of mental illness."

After that, the lama said to his disciples, "Let's go to a tiny place called dMu rDol in the rGyal rong region for a pilgrimage," and they went there. The local king called Brag sten gGrung rje invited them [to visit]. He had a son, the prince called Nyi Ma dBang ldan. (679) They made the prophecy that there would be annual hindrances, and by focusing on that, using the text *Tshe sgrub byar ri ma* [*Long-Life Practice from Bya Ri Ma*], he attained the signs of accomplishment, and by that removed the annual hindrances for the king. In this region there were lots of Bon followers. Therefore, he gave the three-heart *mantra* teaching in the tradition of the seat [sMan ri] Monastery, and then he gave initiations, consecration, and auspicious prayers using the text, *sGrib sbyons* [*Purifying Obscurations*]. At that time he urged them to free life, do daily prayers, be virtuous, and let that be a great undertaking.

A little bit above that region is a place called sNyi Khog. While staying there at a place called rB'u gDong there was a fearsome spirit called sNyi rgyal bSod nams rGyal mtshan. His statue is called rNam 'Jom. The venerable lama went there and made an offering, and because of that the spirit-king possessed someone and came forth before the lama and said, "I am the protector of the teachings. I have taken an oath for the eternal Bon first given to me by the realization-holder, Khri bcun dMar po, and then by the master from the Dre sTon family, bSam gtan rGyal mtshan, then geshe g.Yung drung Ye shes, then the venerable peerless g.Yung drung bsTan 'dzin, then rTa gu Nyi ma rGyal mtshan, dBra btsun Shes rab sNying po, dbra sprul bStan 'dzin dBang rgyal, the holder of the great Bon teachings, the great Shar rdza, and dPal gter gSang sngags gLing. To all of you I have maintained your oath. (680) This time I am listening to your oath. I will accomplish all the enlightened activities [you wish]." Upon saying that, he offered the venerable lama a scarf and prostrated before him. Because of that everyone was so amazed. Furthermore, even his students got support from this [protector] spirit.

After that, a family called Gar ra Shang invited him to a place called rBa mDar. At that time he did a wealth-gathering ritual. From the center, he looked down from the window and asked, "Who has come here?" and sent a monk called Tshe dbang Rin chen to see who came. The monk said, "On the bridge a pilgrim came, put his luggage on the side, and made a big fire for tea." The venerable lama made a ransom ritual, a dedication, and one rosary of the three-heart *mantra*. Suddenly, the fire stopped burning. The next day when they went to see, there were no traces of a fire pit. First he weighed the object for the wealth-gathering ritual and accomplished the practice. People said that the amount of wealth had more than quadrupled.

After that, he went to dKra' shis's house and did an extensive consecration of the refuge objects there. While doing that, while throwing the offering flowers and grains, one of the offering grains remained stuck on the refuge object. Even today we can see this.

After that, out of faith, a number of individuals invited him to Nyin Srib in the Brag mGo region. They urged him to come (681) and he went there once again. People from various villages, Bon and Buddhist alike, asked him to do things according to their individual wishes and he did whatever they asked. In general, what he did for them was a long-life prayer, transmissions of reciting [heart] *mantras*, burnt offerings, giving the body [cutting] practice. He also urged them extensively to practice virtue. He generated the intention that they would make the karmic connection and find it meaningful. They came to see him off, and after that he never went back to a family house again [and remained in retreat]. This is all there is to say about this.

Next, [I will discuss] how in various ways he continuously served the welfare of sentient beings. When the venerable lama was young, he had some tendency toward curiosity in his experience, and later he became hot-tempered. The writer of this story was saying that therefore the people thought he was angry and stubborn. If we examined this from the core of our hearts, it seemed he had an unconstructed mind toward loving kindness, compassion, and *bodhicitta*, which was happening automatically. Therefore, to whomever was in need—whether he [appeared that way] outside or was [really being that way inside]—he gave them from his hand whatever food and drink he had. If guests, pilgrims, etc., were stuck crossing a river, he helped them and guided them along. If we examined the manner in which he behaved, he is not like other people, and later when he was in an isolated place and around forty-seven years old, he did the four giving practices.[5] (682) Even when he wasn't able to gather a ritual drum, or water, etc., he would say, "It is not good to interrupt the [daily] offering to the hungry ghosts," so he did one round of the visualization [daily, without the ritual objects]. He said, "If you don't have the water offering, you should visualize a river and say the prayer, and that will be good enough." When generally people asked him to predict the future, he relied on his ability, and sometimes asked them to read the canon and pray. When he was asked about building refuge objects, he had them do prostrations, circumambulations, and set [animal] life free. For the monks he had them do the confession, prayers, and the hundred-syllable *mantra*. For lay people, he mainly had them pray to the loving mother 'Byams Ma using the *bsam lhun* prayer [to be free of obstacles]. For some people he said, "If you don't stop killing in this year, hindrances to sustaining life will arise and you will be at risk of certainly dying." He even used these divinations to change people in the direction of virtue.

Even if he didn't have many students that he took care of, he

---

5. The four ways to give are: 1) incense offering, 2) dough offering, 3) burnt offering, and 4) cutting practice offering to a physical body.

continuously gave advice to the few he had and scolded in a manner like a good father helping his sons develop respectable manners. When he gave them practical teachings, with no difference between how he appeared to them and actually was inside, irrespective of their status, etc., he taught with mutuality and with no distinction between happiness and suffering. Others said that he gave advice like that. Others thought it was a sure sign of his having genuine sincerity in taking responsibility for the welfare of others.

Continuously, every day when he made dough offerings for the accumulations, he prayed, "In the field of the ten directions, filled with precious gems, I offer to the *Buddhas* (683) and fulfill the hopes of sentient beings. May this become the glory of primordial wisdom in myself." And again he prayed, "To all the gods, humans, etc., through my own speech emanating magically as the very language of all others, may all the eternal Bon teachings be shown." These two prayers are as much as we know of what he said. Even for the future welfare of all sentient beings he prayed to bestow the teachings of Bon and give goods, and for that reason this was the aspiration prayer that [manifested] the enlightened intention to continue. Therefore, the life story in his biography is exalted and extraordinary [because of his constant activities] engaging in the conduct of an eternal *bodhisattva*. There is a kind of lay ritual [that practitioners do] called "doing the welfare of sentient beings." These [if done too early in practice actually] diminish virtue practice and obscure the meditation experiences and realizations. Therefore, he said, "there is no benefit." Then, for a long time after that, he didn't visit family houses to do such rituals. He said, "Whatever virtues you do, if you dedicate them to the welfare of sentient beings, the benefit will greatly proliferate. Like that, if you have *bodhicitta*, even if you give a small dough offering to a crow, it becomes the great conduct of a *bodhisattva*. Therefore, all the time, you should maintain *bodhicitta* in your heart, and by that everything that you do cannot become anything other than doing the welfare of others." I don't need to say more than this.

I understand that the foundation of the teachings of the *Buddhas* is the community of practitioners. (684) With respect to this, in all directions, he gave advice, made the precepts, did the offerings, and built the refuge-objects, and so forth, so he could spread any kind of activities that extended the teachings. Even if he went to wherever a family was based, he greatly urged them to practice virtue, gave them teachings, and gave the gift-waves of influence. He subdued many haughty non-humans. He dispersed in all directions the enlightened activities of benefit and happiness to all. He possessed the same enlightened heart-mind to benefit all beings impartially. Whatever he did only served the welfare of others. This is the best way, wherein he developed [and enhanced the practice of] those children of the victorious ones progressing on the path. Who else could compare with his guidance?

9.2 Serving Meditators in the Accomplishment Lineage

[Next, I will discuss] how he increased the tradition of the accomplishment lineage in different isolated places. When the venerable lama was around age thirty-eight, in the year of the earth-sheep, he gave some minor practical teaching to new students, but besides that, he did not really cultivate [many new] students with the profound practical guides. At the end of that year, while the venerable lama, the great Shar rdza, was ready to travel toward A Mdo, he got the order to become his successor at Shar rdza's center. Then he took the responsibility to teach. In this isolated place he had less craving, and had the conduct of satisfaction. There he started the precepts associated with the accomplishment school tradition. (685) For preliminary practices he used both the main and back-up texts for the *A Khrid*, and a text from Shar rdza called the *bKa' lung rgya mtsho* [*The Ocean of the Canon and Scriptures*] from which he compiled an extensive teaching, and for four sessions of the practice he compiled a complete text on the close-to-heart practical guidance for the cycle of visualizations, principally for those monks with the sharpest intelligence practicing at the general accomplishment center. He gave a one-session teaching, namely a commentary on Shar rdza's text *sNod rin po che mdzod* [*The Precious Treasury of the Basket*], and also used the root text. The next day he summarized the essential points from the root text and taught the profound essential points associated with the most difficult types of points [in the root text]. With these three he completed all the teachings. Furthermore, he taught the generation- and completion-stage practices from Shar rdza's *Lha gnyen shel sgongs* [*Crystal Egg of the Gods and Spirits*].

Now, with respect to the actual foundational practices, he taught the three—*A Khrid*, Great Completion, and central channel practice—and the close-to-heart practical guidance from the *sKu gsum rang shar* [*Self-Arising Three-fold Embodiment of Enlightenment*], the 100-day retreat on the channel/wind practice, and finally, the profound practical guide from Shar rdza called the *Kun tu bzang po'i snying thig* [*Heart Drops of Kun tu bZang po*]. For almost one and a half years he was the head of this teaching center. The venerable [Shar rdza] Rinpoche expressed his appreciation for fulfilling his wishes.

When he was forty years old, in the year of the female iron bird, he was considering staying for a longer time in his own region. He doubted [this, also thinking] that his distractions might increase (686), so he thought it was better to not go there. Then, he got a summons in a dream and because of that he went to the lower Hor region to a place called Shel Khog. He went to a very modest mountain retreat. Then he went to the monastery at gTo mDa. In an earlier time there was a powerful sovereign yogi who was called g.Yung drung Ye shes. He went above this center and stayed in a black tent where he did four sessions of meditation. This was a place where practice was easy and he got better visions. The surrounding land had good geomantic signs and was shaped in the form of the eight auspicious signs. He thought that in the future this site would become the foundation of a hermitage of the accomplishment school. Soon thereafter, he established the foundation for the [new] hermitage. The monks and the village people built the residence for the venerable lama. For other [students] they built many small houses for those abandoning [everyday life]. He gave the site the name gTo lung Yang dben sMin grol gLing [The Place in gTo for complete isolation for ripening liberation]. At the left side of the hermitage was a wild water spring. There was a monk called dPal ldan. He said to the monk, "Grab a stone from there." On the stone he miraculously wrote the life-force syllable *PHU*, and then made the *Naga* [in the spring] promise to not harm others and protect the teachings. Then the spring was comfortable [for use by anyone].

He then spent three years there with a little hermit [and others] in this not-so-crowded comfortable place. (687) For three years they abandoned mutual relations and distractions, and did only practice, and through that, he said, "all the positive qualities of meditation experience and realizations will increase." At that time, all of their food was donated as an offering by local Bon people. After that, gradually the group got bigger [and included]: Tshe dbang bsTan 'dzin, the sage, the reincarnation of rGyal bzang whose name is Blo gros mTha' yas; the reincarnation of geshe g.Yung drung Ye shes, whose name is g.Yung drung bsTan rgyal; the nun called Rigs ldan bDe chen dBang Mo; and another nun called sNying rje bZang Mo. There were about forty in all, along with others from everywhere gathered by their faith. He let all of them do one year of preliminary practices, recitations, visualizations, and meditation. Again, he gave a teaching from the text *Byang sems rgya rsta pa* [*Teachings of the Hundred Bodhisattvas*] and the *Ro snyom skor gyi khrid* [*The Cycle of the Practical Guide on One Taste*], and then had them do the long-version of mind-training on *bodhicitta*.

At that time he gave them a teaching called *Blo sbyong dam bcas bdun pa* [The Seven Commitments of Mind-Training]. The first is, "By me for the welfare of all sentient beings, I will generate whatever precious *bodhicitta* has not yet been generated, and not let it degenerate; by not letting it degenerate, I will make progress, by this benefitting all sentient being in this life and in future, and come to find happiness; (688) and I will think that I can accomplish all of this." The second is thinking, "I will stay in an isolated place, begging in the villages for whatever time it takes to get food and clothing, relying only on the yoga of four-session meditation, and being diligent in my practice of happiness." Third is relying in an appropriate way on the kindness of the holy lama, and not making him unhappy even for a second, accepting whatever he says, and paying respect and doing service via the six jewels, which make the lama happy, and considering, "I will accomplish whatever I am able to do to make happy my lama's heart-mind." Fourth, "I will let go of bad friends who are not in harmony with the Bon teachings. I will rely on the friends of virtue, and think I will never say bad things about self or other, and I will abandon all the bad speech and criticism that only generates non-virtue." Fifth, "If a critical thought arises toward my lama or spiritual friend, I will consider it my misperception, and think that I will become determined not to show the faults of others." Sixth, "By others saying bad things to me causing agitation in my mind-stream, whatever they do, insulting me or bashing me, then, without getting angry, I will meditate on patience. I will think that this is an instruction for subduing my mind-stream, and I will generate great compassion." (689) Seventh, "By understanding that all the words of my parents and relatives are the deception of a demon, I won't give away my independence to others. To them when they get sick or die, to benefit them I will do the practice to accomplish virtue and make a determination that besides that there are no other means. I will think, 'I will set up my virtue-practice in a stable way on this.'" Like this, practice mind-training and make your commitment.

Later, having relied on these seven commitments and how to take vows, he also made a commentary on them. That is found somewhere else, not here. After that, he gave and taught the four initiations on the *sKu gsum rang shar* [*Self-Arising Three-fold Embodiment of Enlightenment*] and, associated with that, pointed out the meaning of mind, which is the actual practice. He taught many practical guides according to what they wished. He gave teachings on how to maintain the hundred-day practice of the channel/wind practice. To some of them he gave the practical guidance for the inner fire practice, which condensed the essential points as an aspect of the close-to-heart instructions, in a way that made the instructions easy to understand. He gave these out of great kindness.

To those continuously staying in the hermitage he compiled and gave a four- session practical guide. He stayed [living] in a manner that was humble and simple. This was said to have increased their virtue-practice. Some, one or two, who were with the venerable lama for a little while, had not yet subdued [their mind-streams], and some who even had much teaching but did not understand it. He said, "I taught you that much and you still don't understand." Then, he cried. There are stories like this. This symbolizes his disposition toward mind-training on *bodhicitta* from the depth of his heart.

Furthermore, (690) even if this venerable lama didn't develop that many students, to some people he gave the practice instructions from the oral transmission and the Heart Drops, and gave the pith instructions for distinguishing between the ordinary mind and awakened awareness. By relying on these, they practiced single-mindedly on awakened awareness. For some people, relying on channel/wind practice, they were able to separate the brightness from the dregs, and he was able to point out to them primordial wisdom. Some people did an examination-meditation, and a *samādhi*-meditation, alternating on selflessness and emptiness. For some people, the view and meditation of staying-calming and special insight meditation were less important, and they were given the meditation only on great compassion and *bodhicitta*. Individual students got individual instructions.

These days some lamas never evaluate whether the students are suitable vessels. The venerable lama said, "This is my tradition and here we never follow a one-size-fits-all pattern to the mold." This is not an approach of an ordinary teacher. This is the system of one who understands the level of the mind-stream of the student. Therefore, I think these kinds of stories in his biography are surely those of an exalted one.

Furthermore, this venerable lama, when asked for an answer, gave the answer most related to the spiritual teachings. Some of the lamas nowadays, if some person came to them with a scarf and asked for an initiation for a dog, these lamas would give it. Our venerable lama never did that. He gave practices to purify obscurations, but other than that, he never gave the *tantric* teachings in public. Because of that his students said that when they requested the *tantric* teachings from him it was a narrow seal [small window of opportunity].

Around that time, the reincarnation from rGyal bzang gDod (691) told him about a site where the front of the place looks like an elephant lying down. He said, "At the nape of that place you should build a hermitage and stay there." It was given the name Theg mCog Tshad med sMin grol gLing. He said, "In the future it should be one of the accomplishment schools." According to the guidance by the venerable lama, the hermitage was built. One of the deities, the main root deity, was called rNam rGyal, the wisdom deity. Statues were made for them and for many other deities. Then, the venerable lama himself came there and gave a teaching from the *mDo dri med* [*The Life Story of Ston pa gShen rab*] and he gave the preliminary instructions, and then he gave the initiation for the thousand *Buddhas*, all out of his kindness.

He gave a prophecy, "In the future, in the year of the water-horse, go one time to a place called rGyal Mo dMu rDor lan and you will get the benefit of the Bon teachings." Then, the lama went to dMu rDor in the year of the water-horse. There is a monastery there called Brag steng Dar rgyas gLing that had been damaged by fire around the time he arrived. Then, under his leadership they built a new temple for the three—Ston pa gShen rab and his [two] attendants called [rMa lo and g.Yu Lo]. He also did the precepts, and gave a lot of support to the monastery for it to go well. He knew the future, had paranormal abilities, and had special exalted skills.

While he was staying in this isolated place, he gave advice through his realization songs. Some of them I have written down. The name of this song is *dBen bar nyams len la blo bskul ba'i mgur bzhugs* [*The Realization Song that Urges the Mind to Practice in Isolation*]:

> To the great Shar rdza, who is the heart-essence that subsumes all the refuge objects, (692) if we pray with respect and with one-pointedness on you, it will turn the distractions and procrastination of my mind toward virtue. Through that, may you grant me the gift-waves of influence to take hold [of the practice in] this mountain retreat for an entire lifetime. *Kye Ho!* Inside the ocean of bad places throughout *saṁsāra*, even if I were to find the wish-fulfilling jewels of a precious human life and leisure, [immediately] after birth we tend in the direction of death. There is no means to return, like an animal under the hand of a butcher. The happiness and joys of this life appear like a dream. The disposition toward fame and gossip is like the sound of an echo. The multiplicity of karma and worldly activities is the dance of illusion. These have no heart-essence, so there is merit in letting them go. This is the attainment of the very profound nectar of the instruction on ripening and liberation. The ability to do this practice

is in your own hands. Still, if I procrastinate, become lazy, and try to fool myself, this is a bad sign, as if there is cancer in the root of my heart and lungs. Ordinary people fail to see this venerable lama. Even if you were deluded all of your life [about the lama] there is no blame. I ask for all the profound and extensive instructions. If I don't meditate on their genuine meaning, then I am really careless. From beginningless time up to now in this life, there has been enough immeasurable suffering. If I recognize the activities and accomplishment of the final goal, I must make a determination without so many thoughts and reflections that [say] I can't accomplish this. (693) There are no officials above me, and no servants below me. I don't have family to nurture or enemies to conquer. I have no success in business or farming, nor distraction by busyness. Who can be happier than one who relies on this isolated mountain retreat? Letting go [of the idea of a big house] I have a small house, and I just fit in this little square, on my clean soft, smooth grass mattress, sitting immovably in the five-fold posture; how happy is this yogi practicing on his state of mind, on this clear path along the nine stages of this unsurpassed vehicle. The three—*A Khrid*, Great Completion, and oral transmission—are never polluted by hard-headed reasoning. Now I have this direct practice from my kind lama. Those who hope to get other practices are less fortunate. The seals of the generation-stage are an aspect of the purity and sameness of the seemingly existing world. The path of skillful means is through inner fire practice that extracts the benefit of co-emergent primordial wisdom. Unconditioned spiritual prosperity arises when sense-pleasures become a ritual offering. Everything I could want is the inheritance of Great Completion practice. If there are students who are able to follow after their spiritual father, don't expect to babble with too many words. Control your state of mind.

> As in the teaching tradition of the great Shar rdza, the Lord of the victorious ones, go inside the face of this isolated mountain and do the practice.
>
> In an isolated place called Smin Grol gLing during a break from practicing the meditation sessions, I, the son of dBra sang this realization song." (694)

Here is another realization song on the advice about virtue-practice:

> Inseparable from the essence of the three kinds of immortal ones, you are my one father, my holy kind lama. I cry out with longing in my heart for more than your words. May we who are not omniscient see your compassion. *Kye ho!* May we as students listen well, not just to your words, but from the depths of our hearts. If there is anyone who is considering engaging in pure virtue, I will pull out a song like this to condense the meaning of these words. *A Ho!* May we attain without exception the fruition of virtue accumulated from previously to now. May we endeavor in virtue-practice hereafter to have the meaning of this precious life and leisure. Those who do not depend on the lama do not have the skillful means to accomplish the realization. Having offered your own independence to your lama, you must depend on him as *the* way. Those without faith and admiration are without the skillful means to engage the gift-waves of influence. To see the actual *Buddha*, you must generate faith and admiration. The lama is of no benefit if you do not follow his instructions. You must do this voluntarily without insincerity. If you hear the precepts, and do not integrate them into your mind-stream, you must do the practice to integrate the pith instructions into your mind-stream. By depending on ethical behavior and restraint as the foundation of virtue (695) in your external behavior and internal ethics, you must protect the fruition from degeneration. If you wander throughout the villages distractedly, virtue is never accomplished. You must finish

this lifetime in an isolated mountain hermitage. Having the burden of a house is that which dispels virtue. Make your own determination not to listen to those of whom I speak. If you associate with bad company, your own responsibilities will degenerate. Having abandoned sinful friends, you must rely on virtuous friends. All the activities of this lifetime are without essence. For that reason, having reflected only on the next life, you must look only ahead to this, to be free from suffering wherever you are born among the six classes of beings. You must generate renunciation, wherein you aspire to quickly become emancipated. Having depended upon the preliminaries of the *sutras* and *tantras* as a foundation, you must do an examination-meditation of the four attitudes to turn [the mind from *saṁsāra*]. Those who have engaged the practice for their own selfish ends will not attain *Buddhahood*. You must endeavor carefully with *bodhicitta* for the benefit of others. If you get lost in the power of the five poisons, you will become deceived in your own mind. Through that, do not get caught up in the sway of afflictive emotions, and subdue your own mind, or any truth of the three—*saṁsāra*, *nirvāṇa*, and path—will never be accomplished. From the perspective of dependent origination and emptiness, you must come to realize the final fruition. Even the fruition of virtue is conditioned (696) and cannot help you pass beyond *saṁsāra*. Those who practice virtue must hold on to emptiness, without reference point. Those lacking impeccable dedication and aspiration will have little fruition. Continuously never forgetting, you must practice both dedication and aspiration. If you do not take refuge in the three jewels, there will be no agent to protect you. Because of that, you must continuously take refuge and engage in the training. If you do not purify misdeeds, downfalls, and obscurations, you will never meet with the natural state. Having meditated to reach the nectar, you must make confession and practice restraint diligently. If you don't thoroughly perfect both sets of accumulations, you will never accomplish the two enlightened bodies. The assembly of the physical body, life, and its sensory pleasures must be offered as a *mandala*. If you don't do guru yoga, you will never meet with the gift-waves of influence. You must be diligent to pray six times day and night. In brief, you must become a witness of your own mind, and your behavior must be continuously in harmony with the teachings in you own mind-stream. Even when the talk seems good, it has no meaning if not put into practice. What could ever be the accomplishment when self and others are fooled? At the time you have attained a precious human life and leisure, which is difficult to attain, do not let it become aimless, waste it, and come up empty-handed. When you have met with the teachings of the victorious one, which are difficult to find, why would you become careless and not accomplish virtue? (697) When you meet with a lama who is a great master, who is so difficult to find, why would you become careless with the enlightened intention of his heart-mind? If you hear all the pith instructions that are difficult to hear, why would any student not practice them as the way? Even if you pretend to have entered the gateway to individual emancipation, why would you get lost in [how you are seen] publicly outside or privately inside, or let your vows degenerate? Even if you had requested *bodhisattva* vows, why with such sweet talk would you still inflict harm to others? Even if you have attained the four initiations of the outer and inner *tantras*, why would you throw your spiritual duties to the winds and let them deteriorate? Even if you have requested the pith instructions of all three—the *A Khrid*, Great Completion, and oral transmission—to guide your meditation experience, would you become a puppet and not do the practice for even one session? Even if you practiced the generation- and completion-stages, and the approach and accomplishment practices without *samādhi*, what result would be accomplished if you don't recite any of the recitations? Even if you find outer appearances to be beautiful, like the beauty of a bride, would you become a puppet without any inner essence? Even if you are in a mountain retreat and are cast from your rank in the hermitage, why would you again wander around the villages? Even if you have accumulated virtue-practice at least in name, and carried this like a rosary, why would you make what is in your mind-stream only a reflection of your physical body? Even if you directly promise to follow the advice of your lama, in fact, why would you not practice and go rogue? Aren't you afraid of remaining in *saṁsāra* and unhappy? Is there anything good about being alive and bad about death and the after-death *bardos*? If you are reborn in a bad rebirth in the future, how will you become patient? Will you be able to exchange suffering and happiness? What would be the point of falling from a higher to a lower [re-birth]? Why fool yourself, as if you intellectually understood this in your mind? If you knew this, why would you drink this poison? If you were to do some wholesome reflection in yourself about this, and try to sell it to yourself, think again. Constrain your boasting and point the finger at your own chest.

This song is a treasury of promises to spread genuine virtue in all directions. By keeping the focus on these twenty-two reasons, we will let go of the fourteen faults in whatever we are doing. By each of the eight questions, we will organize our own interests. Let us say an aspiration prayer that our minds will go toward virtue.

Many people gathered at the hermitage when he was giving teachings and commentary on the preliminary practices. At that time, it was intended to be helpful. That is when the son of dBra, Zla ba Grags pa, let this realization song arise in his mind. So it was said. Associated with that, he gave them some [oral] advice. (698)

In his later life, when he was forty-seven years old, he had the intention to go to rBa mDa region to rGyal sras gdong. There were many students who requested that he come there and stay there indefinitely. Having had good visions and prophesies occur with those signs, he saw that the mountain retreat would be good in the future. Then, he gave his blessings to this place and said, "In the future I shall need this place," so he built a practice house there. He had many mountain retreats. This one he named bDe Chen bSam gTan gLing. Then, he gave a very clear prophesy that in the future, "this will become one of the places to continue the practices of the accomplishment lineage." It remained for a long time. Since he first came there his heart-felt students, the yogis Tshul khrims 'Od zer, sMon lam gTsug phun, and those [other] students who trusted him, said he gave them the oral transmission of the *Dri med* [*Stainless*] and the *Khams chen* [*Great Realm*]. They were very satisfied.

After that, the students had the wish to establish a school of accomplishment. Everybody agreed, and they made the request. Because of that he extended his kindness by giving the *A Khrid* teachings and the extensive visualization practice from the *bKa' lung rgya mtsho* [*Ocean of the Canon and Scriptures*]. (700) By relying on the stages of meditation for the accumulations and purification there are twenty individual steps. After that, the four initiations from the Great Completion *sKu gsum rang shar* [*Self-Arising Three-fold Embodiment of Enlightenment*] were given. First, he gave the four initiations, and then for the actual practice [he gave both] the old and new versions of the pointing out system. He also gave the practice of inner fire as a means to the path, and also from the completion-stages, the illusory body practice, clear-light, dreams, after-death states, and so forth. He gave all these completely. At the end, relying on the teachings of the *Kun tu bzang po snying thig* [*Heartdrops*] he gave extensive teachings associated with these practical guides and practices. Because of that people said that many students got the genuine pointing out. At those times he said, "We are meeting with the gateway of the unsurpassed definitive secret teachings. We are gathering as if meeting at the shore of the precious jewel of the pith instructions. This is the fruition of the accumulation of great merit from previous lives, and we are very fortunate."

In the *gSer thur* [*Golden Spoon*] it says, "When you recognize the after-death state of becoming, then exhaust the habitual karmic tendencies of taking a rebirth in the six realms. When you give up your last breath in the pure realm of the *nirmāṇakāya*, combined with a pure devotional prayer, how amazing! There is nothing left of the future." Even if you are not able to do much practice in this life, (701) if your spiritual duties do not degenerate, by depending on the truth of the secret definitive teachings, in future lives you are automatically joined to the remainder of the path with a pure life in the pure realms of the *nirmāṇakāya*; so you should think how joyful it is to be going to *Buddhahood*. I say this as a yogi of illusion." He said this again and again.

After that year he didn't give extensive teachings on the preliminary practices. When earnestly requested, he explained each of the condensed essential points of the cycle of visualizations of the main practice using both the main text of *A Khrid* and the *Kun tu bzang po snying thig* [*Heartdrops*]. Out of his kindness he gave the preliminary and actual foundational practices every year.

It is said that after that time his heart-mind changed somewhat, and he never gave the kinds of teachings about practice with any elaboration. After that he gave just guru yoga and one or two prayers, and then sang songs of realization. Then, he spent day and night continuously on the yoga of non-elaboration. The first time he came to this mountain retreat, some people from the village and the sponsor came to request spiritual advice, and for them he went to the village a few times, but since he started this retreat he didn't go anywhere, and he only stayed in his isolated place. (702)

Earlier and later, any kinds of things he needed he got. He offered all to the great venerable holy lama Shar rdza in the form of a *mandala* as a tribute to his kindness. He saw this would bring great merit and also as a way to completely abandon the things at hand. First, he offered a bronze gShen Lha 'Od dkar, a statue of Srid pa'i rGyal Mo, a big Bon bell, a bell from Hor, a small double rosewood drum, an offering bowl from Hor, cymbals from China, a vase, a thigh bone trumpet, a reed flute, an offering spoon, gold and silver ornaments for the offerings, a silver mirror, pairs of small plates for the offerings, a *mandala*, a silver hand prayer wheel, new monk's robes, monk's shirts, upper garments, saddles for a horse and mule, a sleeping tent, and cooking utensils. He offered these and whatever else he had, and while in Shar rdza's place, he kept only what he needed. He offered everything—even his cup and bowl.

The great venerable Shar rdza was his root lama, the only one for him. Sometimes if he needed to say Shar rdza's name he would say it with both hands folded in prayer. With respect to others who were connected with the teachings, if he mentioned them he would always do so with honorific words.

He, a person who was a master of realization, always paid respect like this to his lama. A practitioner should know how to give high respect to those highest, (703) and lesser respect to those lower. Knowing this, I think this must be right understanding.

There were two thieves [whose behavior was] contradictory to the practice. He got them to promise giving up their vices, had them carve [*mantras*] on rocks, and then after that he gave them whatever he had on hand. Furthermore, earlier and later, he had many poor people carve about thirty *mantras* on stones, and had them make one million three hundred thousand dough statues. He had them make three hundred thousand prayer flags, each the size of a person.

Furthermore, he gave money for people to do their circumambulations. I wasn't able to write about all those things because there were too many to write down. In countless ways, he relied on being free from attachment and spending his life in simplicity.

Since he came to this isolated place, he sang many realization songs, but it was very rare to see any songs written down. I have written down what the venerable lama has written. Here is a song of realization that urges the mind toward the teachings:

> The holder of the swastika whose essence is the glorious *Buddha*, you are my great guide, who is the supreme Shar rdza, the precious one who dispels my suffering by just remembering your name. Nurture me with your compassion from the expanse wherein there is nothing directly to see. Generally, the ocean of *saṁsāra* is quite extensive. (704) In particular, the three lower realms are really suffering. Here

[in these three realms, because of their suffering] I am unable to be patient for even an instant. If you are a smart person you think thoroughly about this.

We are arriving at the end of the degenerate age. It gets worse and worse with each year of our life. Now it is not like times before. Therefore, if you are a smart person, think thoroughly about this.

Even in the places of the monasteries they consume a lot of provisions, and in a state like puppets they [the monks] end their lives there. Many words can be said but those in harmony with the true meaning are rare. Therefore, if you are a smart person, think thoroughly about this.

Synchronizing the practice and looking very beautiful on the outside, when looking there seems to be a great accumulation of virtue. When looking back into the mind it is like a reflection. Therefore, if you are a smart person, think thoroughly about this.

Right now, even if we have attained a precious human life and leisure, it won't stay long and soon we will die. In the end, even with the precious human life and leisure, we come up empty-handed. Therefore, if you are a smart person, think thoroughly about this.

The youth of the physical body is the flower of autumn. In the end everything changes and there is nothing to rely on. Surely you will see the manner of your own aging. Therefore, if you are a smart person, think thoroughly about this.

Wealth and sensory enjoyment is like the honey of bees. Even if you collect it there is no guarantee you can use it. Look at what is left over when rich people die. (705) Therefore, if you are a smart person, think thoroughly about this.

The mind attached to sense objects is like [drinking] salt water. However much you use, that much more you want to use. The time to be satisfied will never come. Therefore, if you are a smart person, think thoroughly about this.

The three refuge objects we take refuge in will never deceive us. As we practice and find contentment, this is the eternal Bon. The comfortable mattress to sit on is your isolated place [for retreat]. Therefore, if you are a smart person, think thoroughly about this.

The epitome of the Nine Ways of Bon is Great Completion. The teachings wherein the gift-waves never fade are *A Khrid*, Great Completion, and the oral transmission. This vehicle is incomparable with other vehicles. Therefore, if you are a smart person, think thoroughly about this.

Shar rdza is the guide in these degenerative times. He is the treasurer of all the profound inherited teachings. All these [teachings] are like gold and being the same shouldn't be [viewed] differently. Therefore, if you are a smart person, think thoroughly about this.

You should recognize which teachings you need, which are the accomplishment lineage teachings. The final essential point and wish of life is practice. Compared to this truth there is nothing else. Therefore, if you are a smart person, think thoroughly about this.

As you reflect on this, the mind is drawn inward. Give up and put far away the meaningless reflections of mind. I swear these words will not deceive! May this be of benefit to the minds of my spiritual friends. (706)

This was written by old simple Nam mKha' sNying Po while practicing the sessions of preliminary and actual foundational practice. Furthermore, here is a song of bliss from the practice:

Shar rdza is a *Buddha* of the three times. He is the incomparable, venerable, precious one. If we say his name in Zhang Zhung it would be "mangawerzhi." Please sit on my crown forever, as my ornament, [so that] I am inseparable from you. When my mind turns toward the virtues, [it gets disturbed] by many useless reflections. Do not spend a life wanting happiness. If you let go in your mind of all the appearances of this life, you will be content

If you stay in one place for a long time, you will only harvest attachment and hatred. Therefore, do not let conditions contradict the practice. If you keep changing to isolated places you will be content. When you do virtue-practice in isolated places, do not engage expectations with respect to the three restraints. With your own mind in harmony with the Bon teachings, you will be content.

Cultivating the practice of the venerable lamas, you will be content. At the time of cultivating the practice of staying-calming and special insight meditation, at first, don't do *samādhi*-meditation. For the purpose of resolving definitive knowledge, if you unite [the *samādhi*-meditation] with examination-meditation, you will be content.

At this time, practice with this unsurpassed view. Do not take hold of wishing for stupid meditation. (707) Seize the throne beyond mind, and by that, if you cultivate self-occurring awakened awareness, you will be content.

When you recite [prayers] to your tutelary deity (*yi dam*) and deities for approach, do not chase after the drum, the cymbals, or the words; through that know that the self and deities are non-dual and inseparable. If you seal the natural state, you will be content.

When you light the small seed-syllable *A* of wind/inner fire practice, do not expect over and over to get the warmth. To generate co-emergent primordial wisdom, if you separate the brightness and the dregs of the mind, you will be content.

When you are making offerings for accumulations using sense objects, do not come under the influence of attachment to the meat and beer. For attaining the great unconditioned accumulation, if you remain continuously in primordial wisdom, you will be content.

While cultivating post-*samādhi* conduct, do not get lost in an ordinary state. For stopping the delusion of defilements, if you hold the influence of concentrative-evenness, you will be content.

While sealing the virtue-practice with dedication, without mixing it with self-importance, do it for the benefit of others to attain *Buddhahood*. If you do the dedication without reference point, you will be content.

Regarding this long melody of meditative experience, which brings more and more contentment, I wrote it down as it arose in my meditation experience. If you become more and more content, then do it like this. May you get the gift-waves of influence to accomplish this truth (708).

This song of realization from his meditation experience was written by the son of dBra, Kun bzang rNam mkha'i sNying po for his students:

Na Mo Guru Ye. Omniscient sTon pa gShen rab's teachings have three teachings—enlightened body, speech, and mind. If you are able to follow this, it completes entering the gateway to the path. In the tradition of earliest eternal Bon, the heart of the teachings is Great Completion. If you are able to practice this genuinely, you will hold the seat of Kun bzang. The pith instructions of the three—*A Khrid*, Great Completion, and oral transmission—has the enlightened intention lineage, which has the gift-waves of influence. If you are able to balance your life and accomplishment, the signs of the path will happen in this life. This tradition of this holy father and son has the instructions which are the essence of the accomplishment lineage. If you are able to take up this unmistaken path, you will become a realization-holder and yogi. In the tradition of the great mNyam med Shes rab rGyal mtshan, it has the integration of Great Seal [*Mahamudra*], Great Completion, and the middle path. If you are able to take this directly in hand, it is a highway of the *Buddha*'s teachings. The lineage of the great Shar rdza has all the pith instructions without mixing them. If you are able to follow after his teaching, you will have attained the inheritance [of enlightenment] in this life. If you recognize the way, then enter. (709) If you want an aim, then have this aim. If you want to generate diligence, then generate it on this. Without ever forgetting, keep this in the center of your heart.

This yogi, the son of dBa, has a nickname, Gang shar Rang grol. He sang this as a review of his teaching. Using the advice in these realization songs, as the venerable lama said, should [help] you to recognize this as the final testament of the enlightened intention of his heart-mind. Because of that, if his followers also study it diligently, then the sons will likely follow after the father. So, carefully reflect on this in your mind and understand it definitively.

For a long period at the place of accomplishment called g.Yung drung Lhun grub, he continuously cultivated [the practice] at that center of the second *Buddha* [Shar rdza]. He held the foundation of being in an isolated place, and studied the *sutras, tantras,* and so forth, so that the teachings of the accomplishment lineage spread in a hundred directions like the sun. In gTo lung, at the best, even more isolated place, at the Ming Grol gLing center, having relied on being urged by the prophesy for it occurring in its own time, he established the school of accomplishment of the secret unsurpassed series of mind. Isn't he spreading in all directions the continuous flow of enlightened activity? He went to the sNyi region to a center called bSam gtan gling. In a manner endowed with the five isolations and directly relying on them, he gave many profound teachings for bringing ripening and liberation to his followers (710) through the manifestation of his kindness, even at the end of this time [aeon] it is still very clear.

10.0 **His Departure from Life as Rainbow Body**

[Next, I will discuss] how, having gathered in the composition of life, he departed as a rainbow body. [Specifically, I will discusss] how the materiality [of his body] disappeared into light. After having taught, while he was still in his actual body, and having served the welfare of sentient beings in all sorts of ways, additionally, he had the enlightened intention to gather in the [residual] structure of his physical body into the state of original purity in the expanse. When he reached the age of fifty-two, in the water-female bird year, one day he purposely summoned his best student, the yogi Tshul khrims 'Od zer, to come before him. It started by summoning him with a big Bon bell. He had a box of holy objects with twelve objects in it, including the teeth of the *Mahāsiddha*, A tang rTsa zan, and thirteen of the volumes of the collected works of Shar rdza, the text he used for his daily prayers called *rTsa rlung mkha' 'gro'i gsang mdzod* [*Secret Treasury of the Wind and Channel Practices of the Ḍākinīs*], and twelve texts on the cycle of accomplishment and ritual activities. He gave them all to his student. He said, "You take care of these sacred objects and texts. Later, in the future, we, [implying he will come back], and everybody in common, can use them." He spoke these words very clearly. After that, he gave him the hat of Vairocana, and said, "I offer this to you as an inheritance." It was not directly clear, but it was very clear that it was essentially a sign of ordering him to take care of the venerable lama's center. (711) Then, Tshul khrims 'Od zer said, "My house is a very comfortable place, so I will offer you the chance to stay there." To that the lama said, "Just for right now I don't need this, but happily," he said, "this is a very good omen."

I am writing down what the lama said about his earlier and later realization songs especially for those students who were always around him; they should write it down so as to always keep this in mind:

> *A Ho!* The view is beyond all objects of view. The great primordial liberation is the domain of space of the view. How wonderful to be without dualistic grasping. This is the epitome, the king of views. How amazing! This meditation is beyond any object of meditation. The great naked liberation is the domain of space of meditation. How wonderful to be without reference point. This being settled into itself is the king of meditation. How amazing! Conduct is beyond all objects of conduct. The great naked liberation is the domain of space of conduct. How wonderful to be without [the mental engagement] of

accepting and rejecting. This carefree conduct is the king of conduct. How amazing! Fruition is beyond all objects of fruition. The great limitless liberation is the domain of space of fruition. How wonderful to be without expectation of gain or fear of not getting it. This fruition is the king of attainment. How amazing!

What he sang seems to be his final, very profound, eternal enlightened speech [in this form-body].

After that, but not a long time after, (712) the disposition of his mind changed from what it was previously. He became free of entanglement in self-grasping and without fixation point. [Approaching dying] he neither talked too much because it was unbearable, nor tried to hide talking about it. He was without expectation or fear. He was comfortable. Even the way he dressed [approaching dying] did not change. While making conversation, sometimes he seemed better than before, and sometimes he seemed relaxed. Even if you asked him something, he almost could not hear and didn't always give an answer.

One time, he was ready to badly scold one of his students. Then, at that same occasion, it wasn't serious. In the end they were joking with each other. His [outer] appearance and the conduct he did [internally] were without reference point, and he remained like that.

He was fifty-three years old in the year of the wood-male dog. At the beginning of that year, the venerable lama said to one of his students named Khen thar, "I saw a sign that next year we are no longer going to meet with each other." The student wasn't able to ask him why. After that, the students around him, based on the manner of the venerable lama's talking, were unable to understand what he was saying, so individually they did a hundred thousand of the hundred-syllable *mantras*, a hundred thousand accumulation offerings, and ten thousand accumulation offerings, etc., and the *mantra* of long life, etc. They made a promise to do these as a prayer for him. The community of practitioners and the sponsors (713) did the ritual prayers and encouraged the practice of virtue. Then, they went in front of the lama and offered the *mandala* as a preliminary, and they did a prayer of request saying, "for your long life, for you to accomplish the great benefit of sentient beings, and for extensively accomplishing the teachings." Even though they made the request again and again, however, as they were talking at the time, it didn't seem that the acceptance of their request was happening. Then, he remained in a state of being without reference point toward [external] appearance, in a manner busy with the display of primordial wisdom in the state of self-appearing *dharmadhātu*. Regarding his ordinary appearance [to others] it seemed that he remained content.

One time while he was talking he said, "While I am dying, it is important to apply the secret seal for fourteen days." At at that moment, here is the aspiration prayer of his last testament before passing away:

> Original purity and spontaneous presence are my basis, which is the truth of the natural state. Thoroughly cutting through and by-passing complete the skill of the path. Ultimately, the domain of space of the youthful vase body is the fruition. May this direct realization be stirred up from the very depths of *saṁsāra*.

Even when he sang this, the words were not certain, but that year [that very song] appeared written on the wall and I just copied it from there [exactly as he left it].

After that, when he was fifty-four years old, in the year of the wood-female pig, in the fourth month and thirteenth day of the lunar calendar, (714) that day, it happened that he was acting a little bit different than before in his manner of body, speech, and mind, and he behaved without reference point. Because of that, both his students, sLob Tshul khrims 'Od zer and Tshe dbang bStan 'dzin, had doubts [about his living any longer], and they sat in front of him. When the time came for his late meditation session in the evening, the moon was setting, and simultaneously he set up his body in the state of the five-fold posture [for the last time]. Then, after some time, the radiance of his body gradually changed, and [his skin] became very white, like a glass bottle filled with milk, and it was shining with clear radiant light. This [phenomenon] was directly seen by his students.

After that, when they put a small wad of wool in his nostrils, they couldn't see any [external] breath moving. Therefore, they thought that now he had passed away. Then, they closed the bedroom door, and as his last testament [to remain in solitude], they kept it secret and sealed [the room]. Outside they guarded the door, and while doing that they said prayers and did the hundred-syllable *mantra* in case there had been any degeneration of their spiritual duties. Through that, after dawn, the sky remained completely clear, and looked like a blue-colored crystal, without any clouds, and without even the slightest wind. This is how he directly manifested the profound enlightened intention of the natural state and its original purity. The students said that it might look like he was purposely showing off to others [but that was not his intention]. (715)

    That evening at dusk, a buzzing sound came from the earth. It was a sweet buzzing sounding. The students thought the earth was moving [like an earthquake]. Everybody in common heard that. On the sixteenth day of the lunar calendar at daybreak, when they looked above the venerable lama's bedroom there was an arc of a very vivid five-colored rainbow whose colors were very bright. Then, after a little awhile, coming out from the storeroom adjacent to his bedroom were deep blue light-rays, clear and radiant, coming out as if in the form of incense smoke. Furthermore, there came an appearance like the shape of a metal chain with two links joined together, and many five-colored energy drops in concentric circles, with the center circle very bright [and a corona of less bright concentric circles on the outer perimeter] about the size of a cup. Gradually, more and more appeared, and finally, it became a mass of clouds [rising] like steam coming out. About the distance that an arrow is shot, it dissolved into space, just like incense smoke dissolves, and from all directions in the sky, all day and night, rainbow lights kept coming in from the sky. Whoever went near his bedroom [discovered that this proximity] generated all kinds of good meditation experiences of bliss, luminosity, and non-conceptual stillness for them. Similarly, almost two weeks later, a vulture came, made three circumambulations, and flew off to the west, as if conveying a message. (716) We saw the way it was going.

    Later, the lights and the energy drops got less and less frequent. After that, when the students went there on the new moon day, they opened the door and looked in. The enlightened body of this venerable lama was just as if a snake had molted its skin. Except for his clothes, everything else had disappeared into rainbow light. As for what remained, all the hair had come off and the finger and toenails were still on the mattress scattered in the clothes. The root of all the nails had become thinner and longer. We saw what remained there. After that, no more rainbows appeared. It had become like the sign of his staying in equanimity in the primordial expanse of original purity and enlightened intention.

Because of these [observations] I [composed the following:

> Here is the place that is surrounded by a rosary of snowy mountains. Here we have many schools of bKa' rgyud, rNying ma, and dGe lugs. Each [school] is like a snow leopard thinking it is the best one. Here, they are only in a haughty state. Those who follow after the great, powerful victorious one, Shar rdza, through practice of the three series of the unsurpassed vehicle, and by engaging this foundation, will never be deceived. You will be able to directly accomplish the fruition to the rainbow body through the path of the unsurpassed vehicle. (717) This story of accomplishment is like telling a tale, but even during this degenerate time the event [rainbow body] was directly witnessed. Other than him, who else could have done this?

It is said that all three—appearance, body, and mind—were gathered into light. Then he remained in equanimity in the original purity of the expanse. All these—the sky, the light, and the rainbows, too—I think are what he directly displayed to everyone. Even if the assembly of the gods and goddesses of the celestial realms snatched the seeing-eye dog of our world, [the blind students still seem to see the rainbow]. They are like children fooled by [chasing] the rainbow. I doubt that they will get tired of seeming to stay connected [to their lama] day and night. They prayed, "Your Holiness, you have reached the end of ground and path. Through that you passed away happily into the primordial expanse. We are like an orphan left by his mother. We remain, left in this worldly monastery. Even if you, oh supreme lama, have become an object of remembrance, there is no impeding your omniscience, love, and power. We are praying with respect that you get our intention. Will you not show us a teaching and let us hear you let out your breath [once again]? Our only father, who had such great kindness! Even if you remain in equanimity in the primordial expanse of Kun tu bZang po, once again, please display yourself as various emanations [reincarnations]. Through that, please [renew] your action of teaching and serving the welfare of sentient beings." (718) They purposely said that.

A short while after the venerable lama had died, at his mountain retreat there were fifty animals—goats, sheep, and male and female yaks—who all died within a month. I think it was for him to guide them from a lower realm by his great compassion.

If I were to say a little more about how he departed into rainbow body, for the yogis of natural Great Completion the manner of departing is in accordance with the three—best, middling, and lesser capacity. In the *gSer zhun* [*Refined Gold*] it says, "The best is *Buddhahood* without remainder. Middling is liberation of the after-death *bardo* of *dharmadhātu*. Lesser is liberation into the *Buddha* field of *nirmāṇakāya*." According to this passage, there are three capacities. The first one is to depart without any substantial body remaining. Furthermore, from the *dByings rig rin po che'i mdzod* [*The Precious Treasury of Awakened Awareness in the Expanse*] it says, "Here, the way of dissolving the substantiality is that the body that was left by awakened awareness dissolves into the smallest particles, and is called, 'dying in the manner of [the expanse of] space.' While awakened awareness is [still] within the state of the physical body, it dissolves into small particles. Next is called, 'the way a *ḍākinī* dies.' Those two methods of rainbow body [pertain to] thoroughly cutting through practice, namely to liberation into original purity. Therefore, having mixed the expanse and awakened awareness into one, it [the physical body] doesn't come back [and the smallest particles of it are reduced so they aren't seen by others]. Furthermore, [in by-passing] through awakened awareness dissolving into the expanse, the body dissolves [fully] into a mass of light, (719) as if the body were dying in a blaze of fire. Or, the physical body of an awareness-holder disappears [as a body of pure light ascends in the sky] accompanied by light and sounds in the sky. That is the way an awareness-holder dies. In these two by-passing [rainbow body] practices, liberation is into spontaneous presence." According to this passage, some say he became liberated from the former, and some say he became liberated from the latter method. There are many opinions, but, if we were to examine the words of his most intimate heart-son students, like Tshul khrims 'Od zer, after the movement of his mouth and breath disappeared, they saw his enlightened body become radiant and white, with dazzling light. Because of that [report], I think it is clear that his way of dying was via blazing fire.

The reason for it dissolving into rainbow light is also described in the *dByings rig mdzod* [*The Precious Treasury of Awakened Awareness in the Expanse*] where it says, "The essential point of those is to purify the very subtle stains of mind and wind, which are the obscurations of the expanse. Therefore, when these become exhausted in the internal expanse, the substantiality of the external body dissolves into its own place and no longer appears." According to this passage, by the power of the enlightened intention, the coarse substantiality of the physical body becomes clear-light without outflows. Just as the fire burns, by purifying the firewood likewise by it becomes pure. Then, the enlightened intention of the internal expanse directly manifests itself. However, just as a fire exhausts the firewood, even if the physical body becomes exhausted, the mind that continues to serve the welfare of sentient beings never ceases. From the original purity of the expanse (720) again, like an optical illusion, [the mind] is shown as various displays of emanations [reincarnations]. Then, [through his mind] he [continues] to do great acts of serving the welfare of all sentient beings until the end of *saṁsāra*. That way has been described in the extensive Great Completion teachings. Understanding this once again deepens the attainment of faith.

Furthermore, [I will discuss] how, by relying on his relics his followers increased the great waves of merit. All the students of the venerable lama gathered together, and gathered the hair and nails that had dropped away. They collected them into a glass bottle and took them to use as a support to accumulate merit with faith. Then, [in front of the relics] they displayed many great offerings. Having relied on these texts, *Rig dzin 'dus pa* [*Gathering the Awareness-Holders*] and *bDe 'dus rtsa gsum* [*Three Channel*

Gathering Bliss], they made the *mandala* and started the main ritual. Then, they offered around ten thousand accumulation offerings, and with that they took four initiations, and prayed to activate the enlightened intention of his heart-mind so that the essential points would gradually ripen. Those who had gathered out of their faith paid respect to the supporting objects [relics]. They were encouraged to do a retreat on approach and accomplishment, to do daily prayers and virtue-practice, and to set animal lives free, etc. Through that, until they had completed the butter offerings, people from many directions came to get a blessing. Through that, it greatly increased the welfare of sentient beings in an inconceivable way. 'Jog sgon dPon po and (721) rGod chen dPal 'byor, etc., [from many places and directions many great lamas were invited and] they did as many offerings as they could. At the time when rTang mDa' sPrul sku came, he said he got a vision of a clear sign that in the mDo Khams region the venerable lama's reincarnation would appear in the form of a monk, a *tantric* master, and a yogi.

When the offering had ended, the [remaining] supports of his body [relics] were taken to the hermitage at gTo Da'. Then as before, they made accumulation offerings, prayers, butter lamps, reciting *mantras*, the vow to do a one-year retreat, etc. All these became the source of great waves of encouraging virtue. While they were doing these offerings and letting the people receive blessings, on special dates such as the tenth, twenty-fifth, fifteenth, and the new moon, etc., on those special dates rainbows would appear in the sky. From making the butter lamp offerings, special signs would occur. Especially from his relics, rainbow lights would emanate everywhere outside and inside the glass vase. When, at that time, faithful people went to see, in accordance with their own level of admiration, sometimes they saw the [visions of] the powerful victorious immortal ones, father and son. Some saw glorious mNyan med sHes rab rGyal mtshan. Some saw venerable Blo bzang Grags pa [the Gelug Tsong Kha pa] in the form of the statue. (722) Some people who saw these were amazed. Some people saw attributes in the form of seed-syllables, *vajras*, swastikas, bells, etc. Some people said they didn't see the hair and nails there. When some people sat in front of the relics, concentration and realizations arose [in their minds]. Even these days it still happens, and is still amazing. By relying on earlier and later signs seen and heard, through that, for people in all directions, their mind-streams were subdued by their faith, and their inclination toward respect increased.

The lord of accomplishment and wisdom of virtue in all directions, the reincarnated lama, Ke'u tshang Yang sprul, said, "It is certain that all phenomena are interdependent; therefore, whether a cause is good or not, will be known by its fruition. This generation of students are self-grasping to their own school and because of that have spiritual pride." He gave such instructions again and again. Then he went to Shar rdza's isolated hermitage. Shar rdza's brother, g.Yung drung rGyal mtshan, and Shar rdza himself, procured the things they needed to build a *stupa*—the food and the wages. They built a one-story *stupa*, gold plated, with pure ornaments on it. In the tradition of sMan Ri Monastery, a very careful and extensive consecration was done. There were hundreds of rediscovered treasure objects, especially (723) hair and nails of the venerable lama, and a treasure box, all put in the *stupa*. They made this for the merit of sentient beings, and then they did the opening ceremony of the consecration.

After that, at rBa mDa' hermitage, his successor, the holy lama Tshul khrims 'Od zer, sMon lam gTsuh phud, and others, with all the students facilitated all the goods, including a fine relic receptacle made of three weights of silver, and complete wooden blocks of the consecration *mantras* of the three refuge objects, paintings of the deity Kun rig, and so forth. They collected three refuge objects, as many as they *could*. The people of rBa mDa village did voluntary work and were given food. They took three hundred silver coins and made a fine silver statue of the venerable lama. [In the rBa mDa] at a place called sGar pa, the villagers volunteered to build a temple and a kitchen. As for the refuge object, whatever they put inside—the hair, nails, box of relics of the venerable lama—they made a list of these, as was mentioned on the list I used. Whatever they put inside and consecrated was donated to the accomplishment school.

While doing the consecration, many rainbow arcs appeared on the *stupa*. A vulture landed on the corner of the *stupa*. People gave him an offering of food. They didn't need to throw the food because he took it from their hands. People said that these were auspicious signs. Because of so many faith offerings, every year they did an anniversary faith offering for the venerable lama, (724) like offering refuge, purification, and confession of the great vehicle and an accumulation offering to the deity gSang bdag rTsa gsum. They did the sessions annually. At gTo mDa' hermitage there were two nuns, bDe chen dbang mo and Shes dbang bStan 'dzin, who, out of their generosity, facilitated getting the offering materials. The reincarnate 'Bras Tshal sprul sku rDo rje bDud 'dul offered a copper Guru Rinpoche statue, which they had gold-plated using these materials, and then consecrated it along with the three other statutes. They built a new temple there and donated an allotment of money to continue the ritual to the deity bDe 'dus kyi Bum sgrub for two weeks every year, and to the deity Zhing srub for one week. These rituals were first started at that time. Since then, they have continued even up to now. By becoming the seat of [these rituals] it brought the extensive completion of the two accumulations.

After that, if we were to talk a little about what they got and what they did, this venerable lama, first by himself, took the instructions of *sutras*, *tantras*, and especially the profound definitive, secret, unsurpassed practice. Then, not being covered by the stains of this life, he acted in all sorts of ways to teach and serve the welfare of sentient beings. Then, gradually, a lineage of students followed his teachings, including the reincarnations of holy people, and (725) many *geshes*, yogis of the hermitage, and monks, and lay practitioners of the *tantras*, state officials, householders, etc. In this life or in a future life it is certain they will become liberated, or that they have sown seeds of emancipation.

If we count all the ways he was of influence, there are so many. Here, if we count only the main things, we should mention the main people [he influenced]: While he was staying in the rDza Khog area, the lord Shes rab mTshog ldan held the saffron color [as a monk] and was endowed with the three-fold training; the holy sage, the teacher of the teachers of the dBra family, who is called Tshul khrims rGyal mtshan; the holy official from the dBra family named rNam rgyal Grags pa; from the Hor region, his heart student whom he continually nurtured with love, who was endowed with the confidence of view and meditation, the yogi sNyi pa drang Srong Tshul khrims 'Od gsal; from the gTo mDa' hermitage, those who took the responsibility of the schools of accomplishment teaching, a lama called sKal bzang Blo gros. Furthermore, [there are] the students who developed through his practical guidance: the one whose name is Blo gros mTha' yas, who is the reincarnation of rGyal bzan mChog sprul Tshul khrims dbang rgyal; and geshe g.Yung drung Ye shes who prophesized when mGar grong sprul sku g.Yung drung bStan rgyal would be born; Tshe dbang bStan 'dzin who had extraordinary sincerity about the teachings of the venerable lama; the nun bDe chen dBang Mo who is the lord of meditation experience and realization; (726) and the nun with the heart of *bodhicitta*, sNying rje bZang Mo. Similarly, so many others came. Those, according to the venerable lama's order, held the place where they individually practiced accomplishment. Even now, they still cultivate the practice like a continuously flowing river. They go here and there between their centers and their accomplishment schools, too, and they do annual accumulation offerings, remembrance offerings, and associated with these, regarding the tradition of the accomplishment lineage, they cultivate the practice continuously as before. They still do this. Even also in future times, by the truth of the venerable lama's generation of *bodhicitta* and his aspiration prayer, through these, they may establish the venerable lama's reincarnation in this region, and for his many followers his teachings may continue for a long time. By that power, the fear of war and all kinds of natural disasters will become calm, and the teachings of the victorious *Buddhas* will spread in all directions. This was directly prophesized by the venerable lama. Therefore, you should keep this in your heart. Then, after this, if you also keep in your heart the contentment in the teachings of the land of the snowy mountains and serving the welfare of sentient beings, in this place, the schools of accomplishment for monks will be established, and from all your gateways [body, speech, and mind] it is understood that you should be paying respect only with diligence. After saying this [to the reader], I pray with respect.

One day you will come to the end of definitive, secret practice. (727) Through that, the substantiality of the three—appearance, body, and mind—will disappear into light. [He showed] the way of dissolving into the space/sky in a blazing fire. Didn't he depart in the great land of the primordial victor? Just his finger nails and toe nails and his hair, rather than falling, became the support of the ascension of his enlightened body, etc. Again, we make offerings to increase the gift-waves of influence. These relics are the great fortune of his merit left for his followers. Even in these degenerative times, the fame of his name will increase his glory to those who will be born in future generations. In the future, also, the tradition of the accomplishment lineage will flourish greatly by the appearance of enlightened activities.

Like this, there are limitless stories regarding the biography of the enlightened body, speech, and mind of the venerable lama. Out of these, this is how much I know. There weren't extensive records of his biography, and because of that I conducted thorough discussions and interviews with the venerable lama's students. That is how I got definitive knowledge about at least part of the meaning [of his life]. Even so, I was uncertain about most of the order of the months and years, and for that reason I arranged the biography into ten condensed chapters. Furthermore, I compiled this to get a more extensive meaning, so I didn't bother to write this as poetry, but rather I arranged it so it could be easily understood. (728) Because of that, everybody should understand this in their minds. This should generate interest and faith in the mind. Again, in engaging in the genuine definitive, secret, and unsurpassed path, through the gateway that balances life and practice in this life, you will reach the endpoint of the stages of the path of this lord of the primordial [condition], and aim for and take hold of the everlasting kingdom of Kun to bZang po, and then you should reach the final state of serving the welfare of both self and others.

Furthermore, I will say, follow after this supreme incomparable guide:

> Practice the essence of the unsurpassed secret mind series. Reach the contentment of victorious Kun tu bZang po in a single lifetime through the venerable lama Nam mkha' sNying po. This collection of biographical gems is so extraordinary, my mind is dizzy. I have disseminated this bag of gems as an expression of my understanding. Why

don't you fortunate ones take this as an ornament in your crowns? These days some people don't distinguish between faults and positive qualities. Foolish students [who can't distinguish] see the venerable as fake and abandon [the true teachings]. These teachings don't fit easily into some ears, so they [develop] misconceptions. They continuously write to shame others and themselves. Therefore, I wrote an extremely elaborate explanation. The hard work of spreading this has been humbling. (729) These are the words echoed by many of his holy followers. To take them too casually would be unbearable to my ears. I am not naturally intelligent and have limited mental capacity. I have little force of diligence that [otherwise might have] developed some signs of respect. Therefore, these [limitations] might manifest as things being under-emphasized, contradictions and mistakes. [If so], I confess from my heart, and hope that the sages will forgive me. This sacred biography has been the object of praise by the holy ones. With a very bright mind I arranged this [biography]. Through that, by the pure virtue of this, may all kinds of sentient beings take these as the teachings [and] directly attain the *dharmakāya*. The eternal Bon is the earliest out of all these victorious teachings. The epitome of all the vehicles is the clear-light of Great Completion. For this assembly of followers, who follow after the teachings and the holders of these teachings, may they establish a beautiful immense foundation for those who see the great glory. Myself, from now and throughout all my rebirths, by following after the supreme lama as Kun tu bZang po, I become the master of the three series of the unsurpassed vehicle. May I go to the ever-lasting kingdom of primordial [Kun to bZang po]. Even if this lord stays in the equanimity of the primordial expanse, in the future, [I hope] your clear appearance will come again [and you will reincarnate as our teacher] unceasingly. May the enlightened activity extend in a hundred directions with [skillful means] appropriate to all as the variegated play of the all-pervasive *Buddha* fields. (730) Those who follow the ways of this biography with faith, the protectors of the teachings of the victorious ones, Ye shes dPal Mo and so forth, this assembly of protectors, may you accompany me all the time. By the benefit from this, may there be auspicious signs throughout the three realms."

Colophon

This biography of the great *Mahāsiddha* Kun bZang Nam mkha' sNying po, who attained the supreme rainbow body, [was initiated by a lama from] the family of the great Yang sTon family, the simple lama of the snowy land, a great *bodhisattva* called bsTan 'dzin rGyal mtshan Rinpoche, [and] from his enlightened intention he could see the gold in the clay [and saw something in me], so he purposely urged me for a long time to write this. Even though I kept that in mind, it didn't come to me until later. Then, Tshul khrims 'Od zer and the holy sage sKal bzang Blo gros, who are the heart-sons of the lama, the lord of the yogis, paid respect together in front of the enlightened body of this venerable lama, and they very sincerely urged me; and after a while, lo gros mTha' yas, who is the great reincarnation of rGyal bzang, and g.Yung drung bsTan rgyal, who is the reincarnation of mGar krong, both reminded me.

A simple abbot came from the family of Khod spung Blo gros Thogs med. His name was gShen bsTan bsKal (731) bzang bsTan pa'i rGyal mtshan. In the new temple at the center called bKra' shis Ming grol gLing of the uncle and the nephew, the Rinpoche called g.Yung drung bsTan 'dzin, without guessing, reflected upon and wrote [about our venerable lama] in a clear, concise, and easy-to-understand way. Fourteen years after the coarse body of the venerable lama disappeared into light, in the year of the earth-ox, in the beginning of the second month, I started [writing this sacred biography]. It took a little over a year to finish it. By this, may all sentient beings follow after the supreme lama Kun bZang [Nam mkha' sNying Po].

Sarvamagalam. Om Swasti.

PART III – Blue Lotus Flower: The Sacred Biography of Dawa Dragpa

By pouring the gift-waves of influence of the enlightened intention of omniscience from this good lineage, this incomparable biography of great conduct is about how he was directly liberated into the primordial kingdom. The rosary of this story has a well-known meaning to all. At the site of Shar rdza and his successor, as a material faith offering, the block prints were published, which had not happened before. From this, whatever kind of merit occurs, like the splendor of the sun, may it bring an end to the darkness of the defilements and karma, and by the virtue of this, may the lotus of the teachings of sTon pa gShen rab blossom. May all sentient beings catch up with this venerable lama/Kun bZang.

Sarvamagalam. Virtue!

REFERENCES

Tibetan Works

A Khrid kyi ngo sprod rin po che gsal 'debs rgyab skyor gyi gdam pa bzhugs par legs so. Supplied by H.H. the 33rd Abbott, Menri Trizin. Menri Monastery, Dolanji, H.P., India. It was printed at sNyi mo ri monastery in Tibet, no date. (This is the version of the commentary used as the primary source for the translation of the auto-commentary.)

A tri thun tsham chon a dan cha lak che shuk so. The *A Khrid* Collection. New Delhi, India: The Tibetan Bonpo Foundation, 1967. This has the biographies of the early *A Khrid* lineage masters, as well as version #2 of the *A Khrid* root text.

Byang sems gab pa dgu skor. Vol. 216, pp. 1-651, sog sde sprul sku bstan pa'i nyi ma, 1999. W30498.

Byang sems gab pa'i 'grel pa bzhugs so. Vol. 205, pp. 1-912. Khreng tu'u: sog sde sprul sku bstan pa'i nyi ma, 1999. W30498.

Man ngag khrid kyi lag len thun mtshams. In A Tri thun sham cho a dan cha lak che shuk so, pp. 64-117. New Delhi, India: The Tibetan Bonpo Foundation, 1967. (Referred to as version #2 of the root text in this book).

Man ngag khrid kyi rim pa lag len mtshams dnag bcas pa bzhugs so. Tibetan text published in Per Kvaerne and Thupten K. Rikey, *The Stages of the A Khrid Meditation: Dzogchen Practice of the Bon Tradition.* pp. 73-108. Dharamsala, H.P., India: Library of Tibetan Works and Archives. (This Tibetan text was used as primary source for translation of the root text in this book; referred to as version #1 or the LTWA version of the root text.)

Nang pa sangs rgyas kyi ring lugs theg pa chen po A Khrid thun mtshams bco lnga'i khrid rim bru gyung drung bla ma'i ring lugs gsal sgron bzhugs so. Supplied by H.H. the 33rd Abbot Menri Trizin. Menri Monastery, Dolanji, H.P., India. (This is the version of the root text used for comparison; referred to in this book as the "block print version"), *Ngo sprod gsal 'debs rgyab skyor*. In *A tri thun sham cho na dan cha lak che shuk so*, pp. 117-185. New Delhi, India: The Tibetan Bonpo Foundation, 1967. *Rdzogs chen lung drug.* Vol. 174, pp. 123-161. Khreng tu'u: Si khron zhing chen par khrun lte gnas par 'debs khang, n.d. W21872.

rDzogs pa chen po sku gsum rang shar gyi khrid gdams skor. [The Three-fold Embodiment of Enlightenment], Shar rdza bKra shis rGyal mtshan (1974). Scanned version reproduced from a manuscript belonging to Phyug gtso mKhan po.

Zhang Zhung snyan rgyud. Vol. 171, pp. 5-358. Khreng tu'u: Si khon: Si khron zhing chen par khrun lte gnas par 'debs khang, n.d. W21872.

Western Works

Achard, Jean-Luc. *The Instructions on the Primordial A: The Fifteen Sessions of Practice, GuruYoga, Instructions Without Characteristics, and Phowa Teachings.* Kathmandu, Nepal: Vajra Publications, 2012.

Achard, Jean-Luc. *Enlightened Rainbows: The Life and Works of Shardza Tashi Gyeltsen.* Leiden, Netherlands: Brill, 2008.

Bru sgom rGyal g.yung drung. *The Stages of A Khrid Meditation: Dzogchen Practice of the Bon Tradition.* Translated by Per Kvaerne and Thupten K. Rikey. Dharamsala, H.P., India: Library of Tibetan Works and Archives, 1996.

Gurung, Geshe Sonam and Brown, Daniel P. *The Inner Essence of the Precious Pith Instructions of the Actual Foundational Practices for the Fifteen Sessions of the A Khrid*, Book 1. USA: Bright Allaince, 2017.

Gurung, Geshe Sonam and Brown, Daniel P. *Self-Arising Three-fold Embodiment of Enlightenment of Bon Great Completion [Meditation]* (in press).

His Holiness Menri Trizin 33rd Lungtok Tenpai Nyima. *A-Tri Dzogchen, 2004, 2006 and 2007.* J. Levinson & P. A Roberts (trans.). Garrison Institute, Garrison, NY, 2016.

References

Karmay, Samten G. *The Treasury of Good Sayings: A Tibetan History of Bon.* Delhi: Motilal Banarsidass Publishers, 1972.

Klein, Anne Carolyn and Geshe Tenzin Wangyal Rinpoche. *Unbounded Wholeness: Dzogchen, Bon, and the Logic of the Nonconceptual.* New York: Oxford University Press, 2006.

Kvaerne, P. A chronological table of the Bon po: The *Bstan rcis* of Ni ma bstan 'jin, *Acta Orientalia,* 33, (1971), 205-282.

Kvaerne, P. The study of Bon in the West: Past, present, and future, In S.G.Karmay & Y. Nagan (Eds.). *New Horizons in Bon Studies,* Bon Studies 2, (pp.7-20), Delhi, India: Saujanya Publications, 2004.

Lopon Tenzin Namdak. *Bon Po Teachings: Dzogchen Teachings from the Retreats in Austria, England, Holland and America.* Transcribed by John Myrdhin Reynolds. Kathmandu, Nepal: Vajra Publications, 2006.

Lopon Tenzin Namdak. *The Oral Tradition from Zhang Zhung: An Introduction to the Bon Po Teachings of the Oral Tradition from Zhang Zhung Known as the Zhang Zhung snyan rgyud.* Translations by John Myrdhin Reynolds. Kathmandu, Nepal: Vajra Publications, 2005.

Martin, Dan. *Unearthing Bon Treasures: Life and Contested Legacy of a Tibetan Scripture Revealer with a General Bibliography of Bon.* Kathmandu, Nepal: Vajra Publications, 2009.

Reynolds, John Myrdhin. *The Oral Tradition from Zhang Zhung: An Introduction to the Bonpo Dzogcehn Teachings of the Oral Tradition form Zhang Zhung known as the Zhang-zhung snyan-rgyud.* Kathmandu, Nepal: Vajra Publications, 2005.

Reynolds, John Myrdhin. *The Practice of Dzogchen in the Zhang Zhung Tradition of Tibet: Translations from the Gyalwa Chaktri of Druchen Gyalwa YungDrung and the The Seven-Fold Cycle of the Clear-Light.* Kathmandu, Nepal: Vajra Publications, 2011.

Rossi, Donatella. *The Philosophical View of the Great Perfection in the Tibetan Bon Religion*. Ithica, NY: Snow Lion Publications, 1999.

Snellgrove, David. *The Nine Ways of Bon: Excerpts from the gZhi brjid selected by Tenzin Namdak*. Edited and translated by David Snellgrove. Bangkok, Thailand: Orchid Press, 2010.

Tenzin Wangyal Rinpoche. *The Tibetan Yogas of Dream and Sleep*. Edited by Mark Dahlby. Ithica, NY: Snow Lion Publications, 1998.